HUGO'S SIMPLIFIED SYSTEM

SP

VERBS

Simplified

Rules on the formation of tenses

Tables for reference

HUGO'S LANGUAGE BOOKS LTD
LONDON

Ninth impression 1984

ISBN 0 85285 022 0

Printed and bound in Great Britain by
Anchor Brendon Limited, Tiptree, Essex

PREFACE

The greater part of this book is for reference only, and in common with others in our 'Simplified' and 'Three Months' series its object is to save the student's time by giving no rules other than those absolutely necessary. No part of speech admits of greater simplification than the verb, and you will find that comparatively little of the full conjugation need be learnt separately; the order in which we give the tenses allows each one to lead naturally to the next.

The formidable tables in this book show at a glance the various numbers, persons, moods and tenses of all the Spanish verbs, irregular as well as regular. These are merely intended for reference, and no attempt should be made to learn them. You should instead study the rules on the formation of tenses (pages 24–28). By working systematically through these, according to the instructions given, the complete conjugation is quickly mastered. Further time can be saved by omitting the familiar form—which is not really needed by foreigners—and by learning only the condensation of these rules (page 28). A great deal of effort can be saved by approaching the subject in this way, compared with the stereotyped method of giving the complete conjugation without any hints whatever as to the easiest way of learning it.

Special attention is drawn to pages 49–52 concerning the irregular verbs. The peculiarities of these are here reduced to rule for the first time, and when the rules have been learnt you should find little difficulty with the most irregular verb, one irregularity being nearly always a certain clue to others.

We believe that this book will be found a great help to the beginner who has not yet mastered the Spanish verbs, and an invaluable reference book for the more advanced student.

CONTENTS

The Spanish Verbs

WHAT NOT TO LEARN

I. **The compound tenses:** Every student familiar with *haber* can conjugate the compound tenses of any verb, once he knows that verb's past participle (see page 39).

II. **The passive voice:** This is merely *ser*, followed by the required past participle, which of course agrees with the subject of the verb in gender and number (see page 41).

III. **The reflexive form:** This is nothing but the verb itself, conjugated in the usual way, and combined with the reflexive pronoun. The fact that a verb has a reflexive pronoun as object makes no difference whatever to the way in which it is conjugated. See pages 7, 43.

IV. **The orthographical changes:** Explained on page 30, these are necessary for preserving the sound of the final consonant of the stem, and—so far from being arbitrary or irregular—they serve to keep the verb regular. In speaking, these changes need not be taken into consideration; in writing, they are made as a matter of course by everyone conversant with the rules of Spanish pronunciation and orthography.

V. **The defective verbs:** These are quite unimportant, and not worth learning except for examination purposes (see page 89).

VI. **The conjugation of verbs which change the stem vowel when stressed:** These are numerous, and there is unfortunately no way of telling whether a verb undergoes this change except by reference to our lists (pages 53–60). But when the fact is once known, the conjugation requires no learning. It is merely necessary to make the change whenever the stress falls on the syllable containing the stem vowel. This can only occur in the singular, and in the 3rd person plural of the present tenses, as explained on page 11.

PARTS OF A VERB

The verb is the most important part of speech in any language, and should therefore be learned thoroughly. If you are a little uncertain about its general structure, the following notes will help refresh your memory.

First, remember that verbs can be TRANSITIVE or INTRANSITIVE.

Transitive verbs are so called because they transmit the action from the subject to the object. They must have an object to complete the sense: *I find* conveys no special meaning, but *I* (subject) *find* (verb) *the book* (object) is a complete sentence.

Intransitive verbs convey a complete meaning without the addition of an object: *I sang*, *he reads*, *they slept*, etc., make sense on their own. Intransitive verbs can sometimes be used in a transitive way: *I sang a song*, *he reads a book*, etc.

There are also REFLEXIVE verbs; when the action is done **by** the subject **to** the subject (or reflected back), it follows that the verb has the same person or thing as subject and object. For example: *the boys have hurt themselves.*

Verbs consist of two VOICES (active and passive), four MOODS (infinitive, indicative, subjunctive and imperative), three principal TENSES (present, past and future) supplemented by auxiliary tenses, two NUMBERS (singular and plural), and three PERSONS in each number (1st, 2nd and 3rd).

In the ACTIVE voice, the subject of the verb is the doer of the action expressed: *the boy* (subject) *plays* (verb). It often expresses a state or condition: *the boy sleeps.*

In the PASSIVE voice, the subject is the receiver of the action expressed: *the boy* (subject) *is beaten* (verb). In Spanish, the passive voice is always formed with *ser* (*to be*). Such phrases as *the window was shut* (*la ventana estaba cerrada*) are not necessarily passive. If the verb is in the passive voice, the active can always be substituted without changing the meaning: *the window was shut by the girl* can become *the girl shut the window* (*la ventana fue cerrada por la muchacha = la muchacha cerró la ventana*).

Of the four moods, the INFINITIVE is the word given in the dictionary (*hablar*, to speak; *tener*, to have) and is in effect the name of the verb. All it does is express the action itself, without any reference to the action done by any particular person.

The INDICATIVE is by far the most important mood, having a present, a future and two past tenses (imperfect and past definite) all in constant use.

The SUBJUNCTIVE has four tenses (present, imperfect or past, future and conditional), but is only used in dependent sentences as the second of two verbs connected by *que* (*that*), expressed or understood. This difficult but comparatively unimportant mood is fully explained in our book 'Spanish in Three Months'.

The IMPERATIVE mood neither makes a statement nor asks a question. It is a request, order or entreaty for something to be done. An order may be imperative, but an entreaty can hardly be so; the mood is not well named. The true imperative exists in the 2nd person singular and plural only, but sentences like *let us start*, *let the man wait*, are also classified as imperative when *let* implies no more than a suggestion that the speaker should start, or the man should wait.

Of the tenses, it should be noted that the IMPERFECT (as its name implies) refers to an imperfect or uncompleted past action. It can also refer to a continuous or frequently repeated past action. The PAST DEFINITE refers to a completed past action, done once only.

The CONDITIONAL tense refers to an action which takes place conditionally on something else happening, or being the case. Thus, in the sentence *they would do it if they had more time* = conditionally on having more time, *they would do* is the conditional tense of the verb *to do*.

Tenses may be SIMPLE or COMPOUND. When a verb consists of one word only, it is called a simple tense; each has a corresponding compound tense which is formed by putting the auxiliary verb to *have* (*haber*) before the past participle:

SIMPLE		COMPOUND	
I speak	*hablo*	I have spoken	*he hablado*
he will start	*partirá*	he will have started	*habrá partido*
we had	*teníamos*	we had had	*habíamos tenido*

Such constructions as *I was smoking* are compound tenses in English (or rather, continuous tenses), as the verb consists of two words. They may be rendered in Spanish by the simple tense *fumaba* or the compound tense *estaba fumando.*

The 1st PERSON is identified by the personal pronoun *I* (*yo*) in the singular, and by *we* (*nosotros*, masculine; *nosotras*, feminine) in the plural. The 2nd person singular is *thou** or *you* (*tú** or *Vd.*) while the plural form is *vosotros** (masculine), *vosotras** (feminine) or *Vds.* The 3rd person singular, *he*, *she* or *it*, is *él* (masculine) or *ella* (feminine), there being no neuter form in Spanish. The plural, *they*, is *ellos* or *ellas.*

The personal pronoun does not necessarily have to be expressed in Spanish; if the meaning is quite clear without, omit it. However, to insert it at all times is not wrong. The personal pronoun must be retained when emphasized (as in ***she** has two books, and **we** have three*). On no account should you omit the polite forms *Vd.* and *Vds.*; being abbreviations of *vuestra merced* etc.,* they are really nouns.

* See the next page

*THE FAMILIAR FORM 'THOU' AND 'YOU'

In modern English, of course, the 2nd person singular is the same as the 2nd person plural; the archaic form *thou* survives only in poetry and such forms of writing, and in some dialects. Here we show *thou* and *ye* whenever necessary, in order to point the difference between the familiar and polite forms of address, and to avoid any confusion that might arise between *you* (singular) and *you* (plural).

When speaking to one person, the only strictly grammatical form is *thou*, *thee* or *thy*, but nearly all nations have a special 'polite form of address'. The polite form *you* (taken from the plural) probably implied that the person thus addressed was as good as two or more ordinary persons; in English at least, this implication of politeness is now lost. In polite Spanish, every untitled adult of either sex is habitually addressed as *vuestra merced* (*your honour*, *your worship*). When more than one person is being spoken to, the plural form *vuestras mercedes* is used. Though somewhat strange to English ears, this form of address is still heard in Ireland. As ***vuestra merced*** and ***vuestras mercedes*** are cumbrous substitutes for *tú* and *vosotros*, they are contracted to *usted*, *ustedes* in speaking, and *Vd.*, *Vds.* in print or writing.

It is important to note that because of this change the verb, although 2nd person in English, becomes 3rd person in Spanish; *have you written?* becomes *has your honour written?* (*¿ha escrito Vd.?*)

Like the French, the Spanish habitually address children, animals, near relatives and intimate friends by the familiar forms *tú* and *vosotros*. While it is becoming more frequent to hear young people '*tú*' comparative strangers in their own age-group, old habits die hard among the older generation. It is perhaps best that you should avoid the familiar form, just in case some small offence is caused. Wait until you are spoken to in the familiar form before using it in return. Remember the old Yorkshire aphorism directed by an old gaffer to some upstart adolescent: "Sithee, lad; thee thou them as thou's thee, and not afore".

THE STRESSED SYLLABLE IN REGULAR VERBS

When two Spanish vowels come together, each is pronounced separately and forms a complete syllable. Thus, *ma-es-tro* is a word of three syllables. An important exception to this rule is that if one of the vowels is **i** or **u**, the other vowel takes the stress, the two together forming one syllable. Accordingly, *abierto* has three (not four) syllables, on the vowels a, e and o (not i).

Words ending in a vowel stress the last syllable but one; words ending in any consonant except **n** or **s** stress the last syllable. When the stress is not in accordance with this rule, an acute accent is placed over the stressed vowel.

In the regular verbs, in all tenses except the present, the stress is on the first syllable following the stem of the infinitive. But in the future and conditional, the infinitive is used as the stem; the stress is then on the first syllable of the ending added to the infinitive.

In the three present tenses (indicative, imperative and subjunctive), the stress is on the last syllable but one. The stress must therefore fall on the stem whenever the termination consists of one syllable only. This is the case throughout the singular, and in the 3rd person plural. Note, however:

(a) In the 1st person plural, the termination consists of two syllables, therefore the first syllable of the termination takes the stress.
(b) The stress in the 2nd person plural, indicative and subjunctive, is on the last syllable. Being irregular, it is indicated by an accent.
(c) The stress in the 2nd person plural of the imperative is regular.

When this principle is realized, it will be seen that many verbs are not so irregular as they might appear at first sight. The present indicative of *querer* and *poder*, for instance, are no more irregular than those of *perder* and *mover*.

Auxiliary Verbs

WHEN TO USE HABER, TENER, SER, ESTAR

The auxiliary verbs **haber, tener, ser** and **estar** are very important; although irregular, they should be thoroughly learnt before all other verbs, regular and irregular.

Many students find confusing the fact that *to have* and *to be* can each be translated by two different verbs in Spanish. The following notes, taken from our grammar book 'Spanish in Three Months', should help defeat this difficulty.

1. Tener (*to have*) is used as a principal verb, and really means *to hold, to possess.*

2. Haber (*to have*) is used only as an auxiliary, i.e. to form the compound tenses of other verbs. It must therefore precede a past participle;

I have a house	(*yo*) *tengo una casa*
I have seen a house	(*yo*) *he visto una casa*

3. Estar (*to be*) is used in speaking of any **temporary** condition or action, or of the place in which a person or thing is:

he is at the door	*está a la puerta*
we are speaking	*estamos hablando*
I am here	*estoy aquí*
they are not busy	*no están ocupados*

Use *estar* before any present participle, as the phrase then expresses what one is doing at the time only:

I am smoking	*estoy fumando*

Always use *estar* to express **place**, no matter how long the person or thing has been in the place referred to. It is almost equivalent to *stand*:

Madrid is in Castile (= stands in Castile)	*Madrid está en Castilla*

4. Ser (*to be*) is used in speaking of a **permanent** state or condition, a profession or calling, or a natural characteristic:

am I tall?	*¿soy yo alto?*
he is not English	*no es inglés*
the paper is white	*el papel es blanco*
they are soldiers	*son soldados*
he is the manager	*es el gerente*

Property in (i.e. possession of) anything is always expressed by *ser*; the passive voice also requires *ser*:

this book is mine	*este libro es mío*
he is loved	*es amado*

Remember, always use *ser* unless the action or condition spoken of must necessarily by its nature be temporary.

HOW TO TRANSLATE ENGLISH AUXILIARIES

Used as auxiliary verbs, *querer* expresses desire, willingness, or inclination; *poder* expresses ability, and *deber* duty or compulsion.

can, could, be able to (*poder*)

Can (or sometimes **may**) is translated by the present tense of *poder*; **could**, when meaning **was able to**, by the past of *poder* (imperfect, perfect or past definite):

he cannot understand you	*no puede comprenderle*
may I keep this?	*¿puedo guardar esto?*
we could not find it	*no pudimos hallarlo*
they could hear the noise	*podían oir el ruido*

Could, meaning **should** (or **would**) **be able to**, is rendered by the conditional of *poder*:

could you help me this evening?	*¿podría* Vd. ayudarme esta noche?*
they could not (= would not be able to) finish it in time	*no podrían* acabarlo a tiempo*

* As this is equivalent to 'will be able to', *podrá* and *podrán* might be substituted in such sentences.

When **can, could, shall be able to**, etc. refer to an accomplishment that has to be acquired, *saber* is used instead of *poder*:

can you swim? (= do you know how)	*¿sabe Vd. nadar?*
they were neither able to read nor write	*no sabían ni leer ni escribir*

shall, will, should, would

In the future and conditional, the English auxiliaries are *shall, should* in the 1st person and *will, would* in the 2nd and 3rd persons. If this distinction is not observed, the meaning is sometimes entirely altered. For instance, *I shall go there tomorrow, and he will come too* simply expresses futurity. The Spanish future tense is therefore used: *Iré allí mañana, y él vendrá también.* But in *I will go there tomorrow, and he shall come too*, the *will* expresses intention and the *shall* a certain amount of compulsion. The Spanish is therefore *Quiero ir allí mañana, y él deberá venir también.*

The future tense must only be used in Spanish when nothing beyond futurity is intended to be expressed, and the conditional only when an action is referred to as taking place conditionally on something else happening. When *shall, will, should* and *would* have another meaning, an auxiliary verb must be used.

Would, meaning **was willing to, wanted to**, is rendered by a past tense of *querer*; if it means **would be willing to,** or **would like to**, use the conditional or *querer*:

he would not (= refused to) obey me yesterday	*no quería* (or *quiso*) *obedecerme ayer*
he would not obey me in future	*no querría obedecerme en lo futuro*

The conditional subjunctive of *querer* is less strong:

he would not like to contradict me	*no quisiera contradecirme*

must, am to, have to, etc. (*deber, tener que, haber de*)

Must is rendered by the present of *deber*:

I am to go out (= it is my duty to)	*debo salir*
you must have forgotten it	*Vd. debe haberlo olvidado*

Any tense of *deber* can be used in the same signification:

I shall have to do it, it will be the right thing for me to do it	*deberé hacerlo*

Compulsion is expressed more strongly and emphatically by *tener que*, *haber de*, as the following examples show:

I must go out, I have to go out	*he de salir, tengo que salir*
you must wait, you have got to wait	*Vd. tiene que aguardar, Vd. ha de aguardar, Vd. debe aguardar*
I had to do it, I was obliged, compelled, forced to do it	*debí hacerlo, tenía que hacerlo, hube de hacerlo, tuve que hacerlo*
I shall have to do it, I shall be obliged to do it	*tendré que hacerlo*, or (less emphatic) *habré de hacerlo*

ought to, should meaning **ought to**

Ought to is rendered by the conditional (indicative or subjunctive) of *deber*:

he ought to do it now	*debería hacerlo ahora*
I ought to do it tomorrow, but I shall not have time	*debiera hacerlo mañana, pero no tendré tiempo*

Ought to have is translated by the compound conditional of *deber*:

I ought to have done it yesterday (= should-have ought-to do it)	*hubiera debido hacerlo ayer*

Acabar, *volver*, *servirse* are three verbs which can be used as auxiliaries, and the following important idiomatic forms should be noted:

I have just done it	*acabo de hacerlo* (lit., I finish to do it)
he has just arrived	*acaba de llegar*
do it again	*vuelva Vd. a hacerlo* (lit., return to do it)
please answer me	*sírvase Vd. contestarme* (lit., serve yourself)
he doesn't want to copy the letter again	*no quiere volver a copiar la carta*

CONJUGATION OF AUXILIARY VERBS

haber *to have*

PRESENT PARTICIPLE: *having* habiendo PAST PARTICIPLE: *had* habido

INDICATIVE MOOD

PRESENT TENSE

I have	yo he	*we have*	nosotros (-as) hemos
*thou hast**	tú has	*ye have**	vosotros (-as) habéis
you have	Vd. ha	*you have*	Vds. han
he (she) has	él (ella) ha	*they have*	ellos (ellas) han

* See page 10 (familiar form). We omit some pronouns in other tenses, where space is limited (*Vd.* and *Vds.* obligatory—page 9).

IMPERFECT

I had	yo había	*we had*	nosotros habíamos
thou hadst	tú habías	*ye had*	vosotros habíais
you had	Vd. había	*you had*	Vds. habían
he had	él había	*they had*	ellos habían

PAST DEFINITE

I had	yo hube	*we had*	nosotros hubimos
thou hadst	tú hubiste	*ye had*	vosotros hubisteis
you had	Vd. hubo	*you had*	Vds. hubieron
he had	él hubo	*they had*	ellos hubieron

FUTURE

I shall have	yo habré	*we shall have*	nosotros habremos
thou wilt have	tú habrás	*ye will have*	vosotros habréis
you will have	Vd. habrá	*you will have*	Vds. habrán
he will have	él habrá	*they will have*	ellos habrán

CONDITIONAL

I should have	habría	*we should have*	habríamos
thou would have	habrías	*ye would have*	habríais
you would have	Vd. habría	*you would have*	Vds. habrían
he would have	habría	*they would have*	habrían

IMPERATIVE MOOD

have (polite)	haya Vd.	*have (polite, pl.)*	hayan Vds.
have (familiar)	hé	*have (fam., pl.)*	habed

OTHER PERSONS NOT STRICTLY IMPERATIVE

let us have	hayamos (nosotros, -as)
let him (her) have	haya (el, ella)
let them have	hayan (ellos, -as)

SUBJUNCTIVE MOOD

Usually prefaced by *that* or *if* in English, *que* in Spanish

PRESENT

I have	haya	*we have*	hayamos
thou have	hayas	*ye have*	hayáis
you have	Vd. haya	*you have*	Vds. hayan
he have	haya	*they have*	hayan

IMPERFECT

I had	hubiese	*we had*	hubiésemos
thou hadst	hubieses	*ye had*	hubieseis
you had	Vd. hubiese	*you had*	Vds. hubiesen
he had	hubiese	*they had*	hubiesen

FUTURE

I shall have	hubiere	*we shall have*	hubiéremos
thou wilt have	hubieres	*ye will have*	hubiereis
you will have	Vd. hubiere	*you will have*	Vds. hubieren
he will have	hubiere	*they will have*	hubieren

CONDITIONAL

I should have	hubiera	*we should have*	hubiéramos
thou would have	hubieras	*ye would have*	hubierais
you would have	Vd. hubiera	*you would have*	Vds. hubieran
he would have	hubiera	*they would have*	hubieran

tener *to have*

PRESENT PARTICIPLE: *having* teniendo PAST PARTICIPLE: *had* tenido

INDICATIVE MOOD

PRESENT TENSE

I have	yo tengo	*we have*	nosotros (-as) tenemos
*thou hast**	tú tienes	*ye have**	vosotros (-as) tenéis
you have	Vd. tiene	*you have*	Vds. tienen
he (she) has	él (ella) tiene	*they have*	ellos (ellas) tienen

* See page 10 (familiar form). We omit some pronouns in other tenses, where space is limited (*Vd.* and *Vds.* obligatory—page 9).

IMPERFECT

*I had**	yo tenía	*we had*	nosotros teníamos
thou hadst	tú tenías	*ye had*	vosotros teníais
you had	Vd. tenía	*you had*	Vds. tenían
he had	él tenía	*they had*	ellos tenían

* Or *I was having* or *used to have*, etc.

PAST DEFINITE

I had	yo tuve	*we had*	nosotros tuvimos
thou hadst	tú tuviste	*ye had*	vosotros tuvisteis
you had	Vd. tuvo	*you had*	Vds. tuvieron
he had	él tuvo	*they had*	ellos tuvieron

FUTURE

I shall have	yo tendré	*we shall have*	nosotros tendremos
thou wilt have	tú tendrás	*ye will have*	vosotros tendréis
you will have	Vd. tendrá	*you will have*	Vds. tendrán
he will have	él tendrá	*they will have*	ellos tendrán

CONDITIONAL

I should have	tendría	*we should have*	tendríamos
thou would have	tendrías	*ye would have*	tendríais
you would have	Vd. tendría	*you would have*	Vds. tendrían
he would have	tendría	*they would have*	ellos tendrían

IMPERATIVE MOOD

have (*polite*)	tenga Vd.	(*polite, pl.*)	tengan Vds.
have (*familiar*)	ten	(*familiar, pl.*)	tened

OTHER PERSONS NOT STRICTLY IMPERATIVE

let us have	tengamos (nosotros, -as)
let him (*her*) *have*	tenga (él, ella)
let them have	tengan (ellos, -as)

SUBJUNCTIVE MOOD

Usually prefaced by *that* or *if* in English, *que* in Spanish

PRESENT

I have	tenga	*we have*	tengamos
thou have	tengas	*ye have*	tengáis
you have	Vd. tenga	*you have*	Vds. tengan
he have	tenga	*they have*	tengan

IMPERFECT

I had	tuviese	*we had*	tuviésemos
thou hadst	tuvieses	*ye had*	tuvieseis
you had	Vd. tuviese	*you had*	Vds. tuviesen
he had	tuviese	*they had*	tuviesen

FUTURE

I shall have	tuviere	*we shall have*	tuviéremos
thou wilt have	tuvieres	*ye will have*	tuviereis
you will have	Vd. tuviere	*you will have*	Vds. tuvieren
he will have	tuviere	*they will have*	tuvieren

CONDITIONAL

I should have	tuviera	*we should have*	tuviéramos
thou would have	tuvieras	*ye would have*	tuvierais
you would have	Vd. tuviera	*you would have*	Vds. tuvieran
he would have	tuviera	*they would have*	tuvieran

ser *to be*

PRESENT PARTICIPLE: *being* siendo PAST PARTICIPLE: *been* sido

INDICATIVE MOOD

PRESENT TENSE

I am	yo soy	*we are*	nosotros (-as) somos
*thou art**	tú eres	*ye are**	vosotros (-as) sois
you are	Vd. es	*you are*	Vds. son
he (she) is	él (ella) es	*they are*	ellos (-as) son

* See page 10 (familiar form). We omit some pronouns in other tenses, where space is limited (*Vd.* and *Vds.* obligatory—page 9).

IMPERFECT

*I was**	yo era	*we were*	nosotros éramos
thou wast	tú eras	*ye were*	vosotros erais
you were	Vd. era	*you were*	Vds. eran
he was	él era	*they were*	ellos eran

* Or *I was being* or *used to be*, etc.

PAST DEFINITE

I was	yo fui	*we were*	nosotros fuimos
thou wast	tú fuiste	*ye were*	vosotros fuisteis
you were	Vd. fue	*you were*	Vds. fueron
he was	él fue	*they were*	ellos fueron

FUTURE

I shall be	yo seré	*we shall be*	nosotros seremos
thou wilt be	tú serás	*ye will be*	vosotros seréis
you will be	Vd. será	*you will be*	Vds. serán
he will be	él será	*they will be*	ellos serán

CONDITIONAL

I should be	sería	*we should be*	seríamos
thou would be	serías	*ye would be*	seríais
you would be	Vd. sería	*you would be*	Vds. serían
he would be	sería	*they would be*	serían

IMPERATIVE MOOD

be (polite)	sea Vd.	*(polite, pl.)*	sean Vds.
be (familiar)	sé	*(familiar, pl.)*	sed

OTHER PERSONS NOT STRICTLY IMPERATIVE

let us be	seamos (nosotros, -as)
let him (her) be	sea (él, ella)
let them be	sean (ellos, ellas)

SUBJUNCTIVE MOOD

Usually prefaced by *that* or *if* in English, *que* in Spanish

PRESENT

I be	sea	*we be*	seamos
thou be	seas	*ye be*	seáis
you be	Vd. sea	*you be*	Vds. sean
he be	sea	*they be*	sean

IMPERFECT

I were	fuese	*we were*	fuésemos
thou wert	fueses	*ye were*	fueseis
you were	Vd. fuese	*you were*	Vds. fuesen
he were	fuese	*they were*	fuesen

FUTURE

I shall be	fuere	*we shall be*	fuéremos
thou wilt be	fueres	*ye will be*	fuereis
you will be	Vd. fuere	*you will be*	Vds. fueren
he will be	fuere	*they will be*	fueren

CONDITIONAL

I should be	fuera	*we should be*	fuéramos
thou would be	fueras	*ye would be*	fuerais
you would be	Vd. fuera	*you would be*	Vds. fueran
he would be	fuera	*they would be*	fueran

estar *to be*

PRESENT PARTICIPLE: *being* estando PAST PARTICIPLE: *been* estado

INDICATIVE MOOD

PRESENT TENSE

I am	yo estoy	*we are*	nosotros (-as) estamos
*thou art**	tú estás	*ye are**	vosotros (-as) estáis
you are	Vd. está	*you are*	Vds. están
he (she) is	él (ella) está	*they are*	ellos (-as) están

* See page 10 (familiar form). We omit some pronouns in other tenses, where space is limited (*Vd.* and *Vds.* obligatory—page 9).

IMPERFECT

*I was**	yo estaba	*we are*	nosotros estábamos
thou wast	tú estabas	*ye were*	vosotros estabais
you were	Vd. estaba	*you were*	Vds. estaban
he was	él estaba	*they were*	ellos estaban

* Or *I was being* or *used to be*, etc.

PAST DEFINITE

I was	yo estuve	*we were*	nosotros estuvimos
thou wast	tú estuviste	*ye were*	vosotros estuvisteis
you were	Vd. estuvo	*you were*	Vds. estuvieron
he was	él estuvo	*they were*	ellos estuvieron

FUTURE

I shall be	yo estaré	*we shall be*	nosotros estaremos
thou wilt be	tú estarás	*ye will be*	vosotros estaréis
you will be	Vd. estará	*you will be*	Vds. estarán
he will be	él estará	*they will be*	ellos estarán

CONDITIONAL

I should be	estaría	*we should be*	estaríamos
thou would be	estarías	*ye would be*	estaríais
you would be	Vd. estaría	*you would be*	Vds. estarían
he would be	estaría	*they would be*	estarían

IMPERATIVE MOOD

be (polite)	esté Vd.	*(polite, pl.)*	estén Vds.
be (familiar)	está	*(familiar, pl.)*	estad

OTHER PERSONS NOT STRICTLY IMPERATIVE

let us be	estemos (nosotros, -as)
let him (her) be	esté (él, ella)
let them be	estén (ellos, ellas)

SUBJUNCTIVE MOOD

Usually prefaced by *that* or *if* in English, *que* in Spanish

PRESENT

I be	esté	*we be*	estemos
thou be	estés	*ye be*	estéis
you be	Vd. esté	*you be*	Vds. estén
he be	esté	*they be*	estén

IMPERFECT

I were	estuviese	*we were*	estuviésemos
thou wert	estuvieses	*ye were*	estuvieseis
you were	Vd. estuviese	*you were*	Vds. estuviesen
he were	estuviese	*they were*	estuviesen

FUTURE

I shall be	estuviere	*we shall be*	estuviéremos
thou wilt be	estuvieres	*ye will be*	estuviereis
you will be	Vd. estuviere	*you will be*	Vds. estuvieren
he will be	estuviere	*they will be*	estuvieren

CONDITIONAL

I should be	estuviera	*we should be*	estuviéramos
thou would be	estuvieras	*ye would be*	estuvierais
you would be	Vd. estuviera	*you would be*	Vds. estuvieran
he would be	estuviera	*they would be*	estuvieran

Regular Verbs

HOW TO LEARN THEM QUICKLY

The complete conjugations given on pages 32–37 are for reference only; there is no need to learn these formidable tables by heart, in the old fashioned way. The rational, commonsense method is to study one tense at a time, in the natural order, and learn a few simple rules which show how each new tense can be formed from the one already learnt. These rules now follow, with additional notes on usage of some tenses where needed.

FORMATION OF TENSES

1. Spanish regular verbs are divided into three conjugations, the infinitives of which end respectively in **-ar**, **-er** and **-ir**. The part of the verb which precedes the termination *-ar*, *-er* or *-ir* of the infinitive is called the stem. Although usually known as the 1st, 2nd and 3rd conjugations, we prefer to call them '*-ar* verbs', '*-er* verbs' and '*-ir* verbs'.

2. PRESENT PARTICIPLE: In *-ar* verbs the present participle is formed by adding **-ando** to the stem; in *-er* and *-ir* verbs by adding **-iendo** to the stem:

to speak, *hablar*	speaking, *hablando*
to owe, *deber*	owing, *debiendo*
to live, *vivir*	living, *viviendo*

3. PAST PARTICIPLE: Form this by adding **-ado** to the stem of *-ar* verbs, and **-ido** to the stem of *-er* and *-ir* verbs:

spoken, *hablado*	owed, *debido*	lived, *vivido*

4. PRESENT INDICATIVE: In *-ar* verbs this tense is formed by adding the following terminations to the stem:

1st person sing.: **-o** (*hablo*)	1st person pl.: **-amos** (*hablamos*)
2nd person sing.: **-as** (*hablas*)	2nd person pl.: **-áis** (*habláis*)
3rd person sing.: **-a** (*habla*)	3rd person pl.: **-an** (*hablan*)

5. The present indicative of *-er* verbs is formed like that of *-ar* verbs, except that **e** is substituted for **a** in the endings:

debo, debes, debe; debemos, debéis, deben

6. The present indicative of *-ir* verbs is formed like that of *-er* verbs, except that **i** is substituted in the endings of the 1st and 2nd persons plural:

vivo, vives, vive; vivimos, vivís*, viven*

* Except in these two instances, and the 2nd person plural of the imperative, the *-ir* verbs are exactly like the *-er* verbs in every number, person, mood and tense throughout the conjugation.

7. FUTURE TENSE: In **all** regular verbs this is formed by adding to the infinitive the terminations of the present indicative of *haber* (see page 16):

hablaré, hablarás, hablará; hablaremos, hablaréis, hablarán
deberé, deberás, deberá; deberemos, deberéis, deberán
viviré, vivirás, vivirá; viviremos, viviréis, vivirán

8. CONDITIONAL TENSE: In **all** regular verbs, this is formed by adding the following endings to the infinitive: **-ía, -ías, -ía, -íamos, -íais, -ían.**

hablaría, hablarías, hablaría; hablaríamos, hablaríais, hablarían
debería, deberías, debería; deberíamos, deberíais, deberían
viviría, vivirías, viviría; viviríamos, viviríais, vivirían

9. IMPERFECT TENSE: In *-er* and *-ir* verbs this is formed by adding to the stem the conditional endings:

debía, debías, debía; debíamos, debíais, debían
vivía, vivías, vivía; vivíamos, vivíais, vivían

10. The imperfect of *-ar* verbs is formed by adding the following endings to the stem: **-aba, -abas, -aba, -ábamos, -abais, -aban.**

hablaba, hablabas, hablaba; hablábamos, hablabais, hablaban

11. PAST DEFINITE TENSE: This is formed by adding the following terminations to the stem:

-ar verbs: **-é, -aste, -ó, -amos, -asteis, -aron**
-er and *-ir* verbs: **-í, -iste, -ió; -imos, -isteis, -ieron**

hablé, hablaste, habló; hablamos, hablasteis, hablaron
debí, debiste, debió; debimos, debisteis, debieron
viví, viviste, vivió; vivimos; vivisteis, vivieron

There being two simple past tenses in Spanish as against one in English, confusion is sometimes apt to arise. The English past tense (sometimes called the imperfect) is usually rendered by the Spanish imperfect, when an incomplete, a continuous, or a frequently repeated action is referred to:

I smoked (= used to smoke, was in the habit of smoking) a great deal	(*yo*) *fumaba mucho*

The past definite is used in referring to a finished action that has taken place at a time quite gone by:

he left for France last week	*partió para Francia la semana pasada*

The Spanish perfect tense is often used as a translation of the English imperfect, especially in reference to a time recently past, and to an action of which the consequences extend to the time of speaking:

I wrote to them this morning	*les he escrito esta mañana*

But no hard and fast line can be drawn between the perfect and the past definite. Just as *I have written to them* could be substituted for *I wrote to them* in the above examples so might *les he escrito* be replaced by *les escribí.*

A Frenchman would always say *il est parti la semaine dernière* and the corresponding Spanish (*ha partido la semana pasada*) is a construction frequently used in some parts of Spain, especially by Spaniards who have mixed with French people. But the past definite is used in Spanish much more than in French, and this use of the Spanish perfect tense when speaking of a definitely completed past action is usually better avoided.

12. IMPERATIVE MOOD: The 1st and 3rd persons of the imperative (the polite form) can be formed by adding the following endings to the stem—note that each verb takes in the termination the distinctive vowel of the **other** conjugation:

-*ar* verbs:	**-e** (singular)	**-emos, -en** (plural)
-*er* and -*ir* verbs:	**-a** (singular)	**-amos, -an** (plural)

speak, *hab**le** Vd., hab**len** Vds.*	let us speak, *hab**lemos***
owe, *deb**a** Vd., deb**an** Vds.*	let us owe, *deb**amos***
live, *viv**a** Vd., viv**an** Vds.*	let us live, *viv**amos***

13. The familiar form of the imperative (the 2nd person) is formed by adding to the stem the bold type terminations below:

speak (thou), *habl**a***	speak (ye), *habl**ad***
owe (thou), *deb**e***	owe (ye), *deb**ed***
live (thou), *viv**e***	live (ye), *viv**id***

14. SUBJUNCTIVE MOOD: In all tenses of the subjunctive, the 3rd person singular is the same as the 1st person, the remainder of the tense being formed by adding the following endings to the 1st or 3rd person singular:

2nd sing. **-s**; 1st pl. **-mos**; 2nd pl. **-is**; 3rd pl. **-n**

When these simple endings have been learnt, the whole of the tense can be formed once the 1st person singular is known. (This rule also holds good in the conditional and imperfect indicative.) Note that the subjunctive mood may be employed under certain conditions, no matter what the English wording is.

15. The 1st person singular of the present subjunctive is always the same as the polite imperative, thus the full conjugation is as follows:

hable, hables, hable; hablemos, habléis, hablen
deba, debas, deba; debamos, debáis, deban
viva, vivas, viva; vivamos, viváis, vivan

Strictly speaking, the polite imperative is taken from the subjunctive, but as the former is more important, you should learn it first. Note also that *que* usually precedes the subjunctive.

16. The stem of the imperfect, future and conditional subjunctive tenses is found by taking **-ron** from the 3rd person plural of the indicative past definite; one is left with *habla-*, *debie-* and *vivie-*. To this stem add the following endings:

Imperfect **-se**; future **-re**; conditional **-ra**

IMPERFECT: *hablase, hablases, hablase; hablásemos, hablaseis, hablasen*
FUTURE: *debiere, debieres, debiere; debiéremos, debiereis, debieren*
CONDITIONAL: *viviera, vivieras, viviera, viviéramos, vivierais, vivieran*

Note that the stress is always on the vowel preceding the termination *-se*, *-re* or *-ra*. Otherwise (except in the present tense) the stress falls on the first syllable of the termination.

SUMMARY OF RULES

The foregoing rules on the formation of tenses, which will enable the student to conjugate every Spanish regular verb in its entirety, should be thoroughly learnt for examination purposes. But for those who want to master the practical part of the language quickly, the following summary will suffice.

1. PRESENT INDICATIVE: First learn the present indicative of *estar* and *haber*, ignoring the familiar form:

estoy, está, estamos, están *he, ha, hemos, han*

The terminations of *estar*, omitting the **-y** and the accents, are those of all regular *-ar* verbs:

habl-o, habl-a, habl-amos, habl-an

By changing the **a** of these endings into **e**, those of the *-er* verbs are obtained:

deb-o, deb-e, deb-emos, deb-en

By changing the **e** of the 1st person plural into **i**, those of the *-ir* verbs are obained:

viv-o, viv-e, viv-imos, viv-en

2. FUTURE TENSE: This is simplicity itself. Add to the infinitive the present of *haber*, dropping the unpronounced *h*:

hablar-é, hablar-á, hablar-emos, hablar-án; deber-é etc.; *vivir-é* etc.

3. PARTICIPLES and PERFECT TENSE: The participles are formed as shown on page 24; the perfect is formed as in English, with *haber* followed by the past participle:

he hablado, ha debido, han vivido, etc.

4. PAST DEFINITE: This is the most difficult tense to learn, and you should refer to the earlier explanation on page 26.

5. IMPERATIVE MOOD: Formed from the present indicative, by changing the **a** of the termination to **e**, and the **e** to **i** or **a**:

hable, hablemos, hablen; deba, debamos, deban; viva, vivamos, vivan

The remaining tenses are still simpler, as they are identical in the 1st and 3rd persons singular, while the plural can always be formed by adding **-mos** for the 1st and **-n** for the 3rd person. When this fact is known, only the 1st person singular need be learnt.

6. CONDITIONAL: The addition of **-ía** to the infinitive forms this tense:

hablaría, debería, viviría. Plural: *hablaríamos, hablarían,* etc.

7. IMPERFECT (PAST): The imperfect of *-er* and *-ir* verbs is got by adding **-ía** to the stem; for *-ar* verbs add **-aba** to the stem:

hablaba, hablaba, hablábamos, hablaban
debía, debía, debíamos, debían
vivía, vivía, vivíamos, vivían

8. SUBJUNCTIVE MOOD: The present subjunctive is the same as the polite imperative:

hable, hable, hablemos, hablen; deba, etc.; *viva,* etc.

The remaining subjunctive tenses are comparatively unimportant. They are formed as shown on pages 27, 28.

9. FAMILIAR FORM: Except in the past definite and imperative, the familiar form (2nd person) can always be formed by adding **s** to the 3rd person in the singular, and changing **-mos** to **-is** in the plural. The present indicative of *-ir* verbs drops one **i**; thus one has *vivís,* not *viviís.* The familiar form is unimportant, as foreigners seldom need to use it.

STEM CHANGES IN REGULAR VERBS

The spelling of the stem of some regular verbs is altered in certain parts of the conjugation, to preserve the original pronunciation of the stem. These alterations are as follows:

Verbs ending in	change the	into	before
-car	**c**	**qu**	*e*
-gar	**g**	**gu**	*e*
-cer or -cir	**c**	**z**	*a* or *o*
-ger or -gir	**g**	**j**	*a* or *o*
-quir	**qu**	**c**	*a* or *o*
-guir	**gu**	**g**	*a* or *o*

to look for, *buscar*; I looked for (past def.), *busqué*
to pay, *pagar*; pay (polite form), *pague Vd.*
to conquer, *vencer*; I conquer, *venzo*
to direct, *dirigir*; let us direct, *dirijamos*
to transgress, *delinquir*; I transgress, *delinco*

These orthographical changes, so far from constituting an irregularity, are necessary to keep the verb regular.

The pronunciation of the stem of a regular verb remains the same throughout the conjugation; in such verbs as the above, this pronunciation can (in certain tenses) only be preserved by changing the spelling of the stem. For example, the stem of *pagar* is *pag-*. But before *e* or *i*, **g** is pronounced like a **j**, so that *pagemos* would be pronounced as if spelt '*pajemos*' (*j* guttural). The spelling must therefore be changed to *paguemos*. Similarly, *venco* would be pronounced '*ven-ko*', whereas the stem of *vencer* is pronounced '*venz-*'; the *g* in *dirigamos* would be pronounced as in English; *delinquo* would be pronounced '*de-lin-kwo*', etc.

The following orthographical changes do **not** affect the pronunciation, but are made in accordance with modern rules of spelling: Verbs ending in *-zar* change the **z** into **c** before *e*; verbs ending in *-eer* change the unstressed **i** of the termination into **y**, whenever it occurs between two vowels.

to attain, *alcanzar;* let us attain, *alcancemos*
to read, *leer*; he read (past def.) *leyó,* but he read (imp.). *leía*

TERMINATION CHANGES IN REGULAR VERBS

As Spanish does not admit such letter combinations as *ñio*, *ñie*, *llio*, *llie*, verbs ending in *-añer*, *-añir*, *-iñir*, *-uñir*, *-eller* or *-ullir* omit the unstressed **i** with which the termination of some parts of the conjugation begins. Thus, the 3rd person of the past definite of *reñir* (*to quarrel*) is *riñó, riñeron* (see p. 63).

Verbs ending in *-eller* or *-ullir* drop the **i** under similar conditions: the 3rd person past definite of *mullir* (*to make soft*) is *mulló*, *mulleron.*

These are really not irregularities, though often classed as such, but merely orthographical changes which do not affect the pronunciation.

MODEL CONJUGATIONS OF REGULAR VERBS

On the six pages that follow we give the complete conjugation of *hablar, deber* and *vivir*. These three verbs are the best representatives of the first, second and third conjugations respectively; all regular verbs whose infinitives end in *-ar* are conjugated like *hablar,* those in *-er* are like *deber* and those in *-ir* are like *vivir*.

hablar *to speak*

PRESENT PARTICIPLE hablando   PAST PARTICIPLE hablado

INDICATIVE MOOD

PRESENT TENSE

I speak	yo hablo	*we speak*	nosotros hablamos
*thou speakest**	tú hablas	*ye speak**	vosotros habláis
you speak	Vd. habla	*you speak*	Vds. hablan
he (she) speaks	él (ella) habla	*they speak*	ellos (-as) hablan

* See page 10 (familiar form). We omit some pronouns in other tenses, where space is limited (*Vd.* and *Vds.* obligatory—page 9).

IMPERFECT

*I spoke**	yo hablaba	*we spoke*	nosotros hablábamos
thou spokest	tú hablabas	*ye spoke*	vosotros hablabais
you spoke	Vd. hablaba	*you spoke*	Vds. hablaban
he spoke	él hablaba	*they spoke*	ellos hablaban

* Or *I was speaking* or *used to speak*, etc.

PAST DEFINITE

I spoke	yo hablé	*we spoke*	nosotros hablamos
thou spokest	tú hablaste	*ye spoke*	vosotros hablasteis
you spoke	Vd. habló	*you spoke*	Vds. hablaron
he spoke	él habló	*they spoke*	ellos hablaron

FUTURE

I shall speak	yo hablaré	*we shall speak*	hablaremos
thou wilt speak	tú hablarás	*ye will speak*	hablaréis
you will speak	Vd. hablará	*you will speak*	Vds. hablarán
he will speak	él hablará	*they will speak*	hablarán

CONDITIONAL

I should speak	yo hablaría	*we should speak*	hablaríamos
thou wld speak	tú hablarías	*ye would speak*	hablaríais
you would speak	Vd. hablaría	*you would speak*	Vds. hablarían
he would speak	él hablaría	*they would speak*	hablarían

IMPERATIVE MOOD

speak (polite)	hable Vd.	*speak* (polite)	hablen Vds.
speak (familiar)	habla (tú)	*speak* (familiar)	hablad (vosotros)

OTHER PERSONS NOT STRICTLY IMPERATIVE

let us speak	hablemos (nosotros, -as)
let him speak	hable (él, ella)
let them speak	hablen (ellos, -as)

SUBJUNCTIVE MOOD

Usually prefaced by *that* or *if* in English, *que* in Spanish

PRESENT

I speak	hable	*we speak*	hablemos
thou speak	hables	*ye speak*	habléis
you speak	Vd. hable	*you speak*	Vds. hablen
he speak	hable	*they speak*	hablen

IMPERFECT

I spoke	hablase	*we spoke*	hablásemos
thou spokest	hablases	*ye spoke*	hablaseis
you spoke	Vd. hablase	*you spoke*	Vds. hablasen
he spoke	hablase	*they spoke*	hablasen

FUTURE

I shall speak	hablare	*we shall speak*	habláremos
thou wilt speak	hablares	*ye will speak*	hablareis
you will speak	Vd. hablare	*you will speak*	Vds. hablaren
he will speak	hablare	*they will speak*	hablaren

CONDITIONAL

I should speak	hablara	*we should speak*	habláramos
thou wld speak	hablaras	*ye would speak*	hablarais
you would speak	Vd. hablara	*you would speak*	Vds. hablaran
he would speak	hablara	*they would speak*	hablaran

deber *to owe*

PRESENT PARTICIPLE debiendo PAST PARTICIPLE debido

INDICATIVE MOOD

PRESENT TENSE

I owe	yo debo	*we owe*	nosotros (-as) debemos
thou owest	tú debes*	*ye owe*	vosotros (-as) debéis
you owe	Vd. debe	*you owe*	Vds. deben
he (she) owes	él (ella) debe	*they owe*	ellos (ellas) deben

* See page 10 (familiar form). We omit some pronouns in other tenses, where space is limited (*Vd.* and *Vds.* obligatory—page 9).

IMPERFECT

*I was owing**	yo debía	*we were owing*	debíamos
thou wast owing	tú debías	*ye were owing*	debíais
you were owing	Vd. debía	*you were owing*	Vds. debían
he was owing	él debía	*they were owing*	debían

* Or *I owed* or *used to owe*, etc.

PAST DEFINITE

I owed	yo debí	*we owed*	nosotros debimos
thou owedst	tú debiste	*ye owed*	vosotros debisteis
you owed	Vd. debió	*you owed*	Vds. debieron
he owed	él debió	*they owed*	ellos debieron

FUTURE

I shall owe	yo deberé	*we shall owe*	deberemos
thou wilt owe	tú deberás	*ye will owe*	deberéis
you will owe	Vd. deberá	*you will owe*	Vds. deberán
he will owe	él deberá	*they will owe*	deberán

CONDITIONAL

I should owe	yo debería	*we should owe*	deberíamos
thou would owe	tú deberías	*ye would owe*	deberíais
you would owe	Vd. debería	*you would owe*	Vds. deberían
he would owe	él debería	*they would owe*	deberían

IMPERATIVE MOOD

owe (polite)	deba Vd.	*owe* (polite)	deban Vds.
owe (familiar)	debe (tú)	*owe* (familiar)	debed (vosotros)

OTHER PERSONS NOT STRICTLY IMPERATIVE

let us owe	debamos (nosotros, -as)
let him (her) owe	deba (él, ella)
let them owe	deban (ellos, ellas)

SUBJUNCTIVE MOOD

Usually prefaced by *that* or *if* in English, *que* in Spanish

PRESENT

I owe	deba	*we owe*	debamos
thou owe	debas	*ye owe*	debáis
you owe	Vd. deba	*you owe*	Vds. deban
he owe	deba	*they owe*	deban

IMPERFECT

I owed	debiese	*we owed*	debiésemos
thou owedst	debieses	*ye owed*	debieseis
you owed	Vd. debiese	*you owed*	Vds. debiesen
he owed	debiese	*they owed*	debiesen

FUTURE

I shall owe	debiere	*we shall owe*	debiéremos
thou wilt owe	debieres	*ye will owe*	debiereis
you will owe	Vd. debiere	*you will owe*	Vds. debieren
he will owe	debiere	*they will owe*	debieren

CONDITIONAL

I should owe	debiera	*we should owe*	debiéramos
thou would owe	debieras	*ye would owe*	debierais
you would owe	Vd. debiera	*you would owe*	Vds. debieran
he would owe	debiera	*they would owe*	debieran

vivir *to live*

PRESENT PARTICIPLE viviendo   PAST PARTICIPLE vivido

INDICATIVE MOOD

PRESENT TENSE

I live	yo vivo	*we live*	nosotros vivimos
*thou livest**	tú vives	*ye live**	vosotros vivís
you live	Vd. vive	*you live*	Vds. viven
he (she) lives	él (ella) vive	*they live*	ellos (ellas) viven

* See page 10 (familiar form). We omit some pronouns in other tenses, where space is limited (*Vd.* and *Vds.* obligatory—page 9).

IMPERFECT

*I was living**	yo vivía	*we were living*	vivíamos
thou wast living	tú vivías	*ye were living*	vivíais
you were living	Vd. vivía	*you were living*	Vds. vivían
he was living	él vivía	*they were living*	vivían

* Or *I lived* or *used to live*, etc.

PAST DEFINITE

I lived	yo viví	*we lived*	nosotros vivimos
thou livedst	tú viviste	*ye lived*	vosotros vivisteis
you lived	Vd. vivió	*you lived*	Vds. vivieron
he lived	él vivió	*they lived*	ellos vivieron

FUTURE

I shall live	yo viviré	*we shall live*	viviremos
thou wilt live	tú vivirás	*ye will live*	viviréis
you will live	Vd. vivirá	*you will live*	Vds. vivirán
he will live	él vivirá	*they will live*	vivirán

CONDITIONAL

I should live	yo viviría	*we should live*	viviríamos
thou would live	tú vivirías	*ye would live*	viviríais
you would live	Vd. viviría	*you would live*	Vds. vivirían
he would live	él viviría	*they would live*	vivirían

IMPERATIVE MOOD

live (polite)	viva Vd.	*live* (polite)	vivan Vds.
live (familiar)	vive (tú)	*live* (familiar)	vivid (vosotros)

OTHER PERSONS NOT STRICTLY IMPERATIVE

let us live	vivamos (nosotros, -as)
let him live	viva (él, ella)
let them live	vivan (ellos, -as)

SUBJUNCTIVE MOOD

Usually prefaced by *that* or *if* in English, *que* in Spanish

PRESENT

I live	viva	*we live*	vivamos
thou live	vivas	*ye live*	viváis
you live	Vd. viva	*you live*	Vds. vivan
he live	viva	*they live*	vivan

IMPERFECT

I lived	viviese	*we lived*	viviésemos
thou livedst	vivieses	*ye lived*	vivieseis
you lived	Vd. viviese	*you lived*	Vds. viviesen
he lived	viviese	*they lived*	viviesen

FUTURE

I shall live	viviere	*we shall live*	viviéremos
thou wilt live	vivieres	*ye will live*	viviereis
you will live	Vd. viviere	*you will live*	Vds. vivieren
he will live	viviere	*they will live*	vivieren

CONDITIONAL

I should live	viviera	*we should live*	viviéramos
thou would live	vivieras	*ye would live*	vivierais
you would live	Vd. viviera	*you would live*	Vds. vivieran
he would live	viviera	*they would live*	vivieran

TABLE OF TERMINATIONS

INDICATIVE MOOD

PRESENT

	SINGULAR 1st person	2nd pers.	3rd pers.	PLURAL 1st pers.	2nd pers.	3rd pers.
-AR	o,	a } s,	a;	a } mos,	ái } s,	a } n
-ER	o,	e } s,	e;	e } mos,	éi } s,	e } n
-IR	o,	e } s,	e;	i } mos,	í } s,	e } n

IMPERFECT

-AR	ab } a,	ab } as,	ab } a;	áb } amos	ab } ais	ab } an
-ER	í } a,	í } as,	í } a;	í } amos	í } ais	í } an
-IR	í } a,	í } as,	í } a;	í } amos	í } ais	í } an

PAST DEFINITE

-AR	é	a } ste,	ó;	a } mos,	a } steis	a } ron
-ER	í,	i } ste,	ió;	i } mos,	i } steis	ie } ron
-IR	í,	i } ste,	ió;	i } mos,	i } steis	ie } ron

FUTURE

-AR	a } ré,	a } rás,	a } rá;	a } remos,	a } réis,	a } rán
-ER	e } ré,	e } rás,	e } rá;	e } remos,	e } réis,	e } rán
-IR	i } ré,	i } rás,	i } rá;	i } remos,	i } réis,	i } rán

CONDITIONAL

-AR	a } ría,	a } rías,	a } ría;	a } ríamos,	a } ríais	a } rían
-ER	e } ría,	e } rías,	e } ría;	e } ríamos,	e } ríais	e } rían
-IR	i } ría,	i } rías,	i } ría;	i } ríamos,	i } ríais	i } rían

SUBJUNCTIVE MOOD

PRESENT

-AR	e,	e } s,	e;	e } mos,	é } is,	e } n
-ER	a,	a } s,	a;	a } mos,	á } is,	a } n
-IR	a,	a } s,	a;	a } mos,	á } is,	a } n

IMPERFECT

	SINGULAR 1st person	2nd pers.	3rd pers.	PLURAL 1st pers.	2nd pers.	3rd pers.
-AR	a	a	a	á	a	a
-ER	ie } se,	ie } ses,	ie } se;	ié } semos,	ie } seis,	ie } sen
-IR	ie	ie	ie	ié	ie	ie

FUTURE

-AR	a	a	a	á	a	a
-ER	ie } re,	ie } res,	ie } re;	ié } remos,	ie } reis,	ie } ren
-IR	ie	ie	ie	ié	ie	ie

CONDITIONAL

-AR	a	a	a	á	a	a
-ER	ie } ra,	ie } ras,	ie } ra;	ié } ramos,	ie } rais,	ie } ran
-IR	ie	ie	ie	ié	ie	ie

COMPOUND TENSES

These are formed as in English, with the past participle and the auxiliary verb *haber* (*to have*), and therefore do not require much study. A reference list of compound tenses with *haber* follows, the 1st person singular only being given:

INFINITIVE PERFECT

to have *spoken, owed, lived, had, been*	**haber** hablado, debido, vivido, tenido, estado or sido

PARTICIPLE PERFECT

having *spoken, owed, lived, had, been*	**habiendo** hablado, debido, vivido, tenido, estado or sido

PERFECT

I have *spoken, owed, lived, had, been*	**yo he** hablado, debido, vivido, tenido, estado or sido

PLUPERFECT

I had *spoken, owed, lived, had, been*	**yo había** hablado, debido, vivido, tenido, estado or sido

PAST DEFINITE PERFECT

I had *spoken, owed, lived, had, been*	**yo hube** hablado, debido, vivido, tenido, estado or sido

FUTURE PERFECT

I shall have *spoken, owed, lived, had, been*	**yo habré** hablado, debido, vivido, tenido, estado or sido

CONDITIONAL PERFECT

I should have *spoken, owed, lived, had, been*	**yo habría** hablado, debido, vivido, tenido, estado or sido

PERFECT SUBJUNCTIVE

(***that***) ***I have*** *spoken, owed, lived, had, been*	**yo haya** hablado, debido, vivido, tenido, estado or sido

PLUPERFECT SUBJUNCTIVE

(***that***) ***I had*** *spoken, owed, lived, had, been*	**yo hubiese** hablado, debido, vivido, tenido, estado or sido

FUTURE PERFECT SUBJUNCTIVE

(***if***) ***I shall have*** *spoken, owed, lived, had, been*	**yo hubiere** hablado, debido, vivido, tenido, estado or sido

CONDITIONAL PERFECT SUBJUNCTIVE

(***that***) ***I should have*** *spoken, owed, lived, had, been*	**yo hubiera** hablado, debido, vivido, tenido, estado or sido

THE PASSIVE VOICE

The passive is formed as in English, with the past participle and the auxiliary verb *ser* (*to be*). In the model conjugation that follows, note that only the present indicative is complete with feminine and plural extensions; remember that the past participle must agree with its subject in **all** tenses, both in gender and in number. The *-a*, *-as*, and *-os* should remind you of this.

ser temido *to be feared*

INFINITIVE: *to be feared* ser temido, -a, -os, -as

PRESENT PARTICIPLE: *being feared* siendo temido, -a, -as, -os

PAST PARTICIPLE: *been feared* sido temido, -a, -as, -os

INDICATIVE

PRESENT TENSE

I am feared	yo soy temido, -a
thou art feared	tú eres temido, -a
you are feared	Vd. es temido, -a
he is feared	él es temido
she is feared	ella es temida
we are feared	nosotros, -as somos temidos, -as
ye are feared	vosotros, -as sois temidos, -as
you are feared	Vds. son temidos, -as
they are feared	ellos, -as son temidos, -as

IMPERFECT: *I was feared, etc.* yo era temido, -a, etc.

PAST DEFINITE: *I was feared, etc.* yo fui temido, -a, etc.

FUTURE: *I shall be feared, etc.* yo seré temido, -a, etc.

CONDITIONAL: *I should be feared, etc.* yo sería temido, -a

IMPERATIVE

POLITE FORM: *be feared* sea Vd. temido, -a (*singular*)
sean Vds. temidos, -as (*plural*)

FAMILIAR FORM: *be* (*thou*) *feared* sé (tú) temido, -a
be (*ye*) *feared* sed (vosotros) temidos, -as

OTHER PERSONS: *let us be feared* seamos (nosotros, -as) temidos, -as
let him (*her*) *be feared* sea (él, ella) temido, -a
let them be feared sean (ellos, -as) temidos, -as

SUBJUNCTIVE

PRESENT: (*that*) *I may be feared* yo sea temido, -a

IMPERFECT: (*that*) *I were feared* yo fuese temido, -a

FUTURE: (*if*) *I shall be feared* yo fuere temido, -a

CONDITIONAL: (*that*) *I should be feared* yo fuera temido, -a

COMPOUND TENSES

PERFECT: *I have been feared* yo he sido temido, -a

PLUPERFECT: *I had been feared* yo había sido temido, -a

PAST DEFINITE PERFECT: *I had been feared* yo hube sido temido, -a

FUTURE PERFECT: *I shall have been feared* yo habré sido temido, -a

CONDITIONAL PERFECT: *I should have been feared* yo habría sido temido, -a

PERFECT SUBJUNCTIVE: (*that*) *I have feared* yo haya sido temido, -a

PLUPERFECT SUBJUNCTIVE: (*that*) *I have feared* yo hubiese sido temido, -a

FUTURE PERFECT SUBJUNCTIVE: (*if*) *I shall have been feared* yo hubiere sido temido, -a

CONDITIONAL PERFECT SUBJUNCTIVE: (*that*) *I should have been feared* yo hubiera sido temido, -a

CONJUGATION OF A REFLEXIVE VERB

lavarse *to wash oneself*

PARTICIPLES

washing oneself	lavándose
to have washed oneself	haberse lavado
having washed oneself	habiéndose lavado

INDICATIVE MOOD

PRESENT TENSE

I wash myself	(yo) me lavo
thou washest thyself	(tú) te lavas
you wash yourself	Vd. se lava
he washes himself	(él) se lava
she washes herself	(ella) se lava
we wash ourselves	(nosotros, -as) nos lavamos
ye wash yourselves	(vosotros, -as) os laváis
you wash yourselves	Vds. se lavan
they wash themselves	(ellos, -as) se lavan

IMPERFECT

I was washing myself, etc.	me lavaba	nos lavábamos
	te lavabas	os lavabais
	se lavaba	se lavaban

PAST DEFINITE

I washed myself, etc.	me lavé	nos lavamos
	te lavaste	os lavasteis
	se lavó	se lavaron

FUTURE

I shall wash myself, etc.	me lavaré	nos lavaremos
	te lavarás	os lavaréis
	se lavará	se lavarán

CONDITIONAL

I should wash myself, etc.	me lavaría	nos lavaríamos
	te lavarías	os lavaríais
	se lavaría	se lavarían

IMPERATIVE MOOD

POLITE FORM

wash yourself	lávese (Vd.)	*wash yourselves*	lávense (Vds.)

FAMILIAR FORM

wash thyself	lávate	*wash yourselves*	laváos

OTHER FORMS NOT STRICTLY IMPERATIVE

let us wash ourselves	lavémonos (nosotros, -as)
let him wash himself	lávese (él *or* que se lave (él)
let her wash herself	lávese (ella) *or* que se lave (ella)
let them wash themselves	lávense (ellos, -as) *or* que se laven (ellos, -as)

NEGATIVE OF THE ABOVE FORMS

do not wash yourself	no se lave (Vd.)
do not wash yourselves	no se laven (Vds.)
do not wash thyself	no te laves
do not wash yourselves	no os lavéis
do not let us wash ourselves	no nos lavemos
let him not wash himself	(que) no se lave (él)
let her not wash herself	(que) no se lave (ella)
let them not wash themselves	(que) no se laven (ellos, -as)

SUBJUNCTIVE MOOD

PRESENT

(*that*) *I wash myself, etc.*	me lave	nos lavemos
	te laves	os lavéis
	se lave	se laven

IMPERFECT

(*that*) *I washed myself, etc.*	me lavase	nos lavásemos
	te lavases	os lavaseis
	se lavase	se lavasen

FUTURE

(*if*) *I shall wash myself, etc.*	me lavare	nos laváremos
	te lavares	os lavareis
	se lavare	se lavaren

CONDITIONAL

(that) I should wash myself, etc.	me lavara te lavaras se lavara	nos laváramos os lavarais se lavaran

COMPOUND TENSES

PERFECT

I have washed myself, etc.	me he lavado te has lavado se ha lavado	nos hemos lavado os habéis lavado se han lavado

PLUPERFECT

I had washed myself, etc.	me había lavado te habías lavado se había lavado	nos habíamos lavado os habíais lavado se habían lavado

PAST DEFINITE PERFECT

I had washed myself, etc.	me hube lavado te hubiste lavado se hubo lavado	nos hubimos lavado os hubisteis lavado se hubieron lavado

FUTURE PERFECT

I shall have washed myself, etc.	me habré lavado te habrás lavado se habrá lavado	nos habremos lavado os habréis lavado se habrán lavado

CONDITIONAL PERFECT

I should have washed myself, etc.	me habría lavado te habrías lavado se habría lavado	nos habríamos lavado os habríais lavado se habrían lavado

PERFECT SUBJUNCTIVE

(that) I have washed myself, etc.	me haya lavado te hayas lavado se haya lavado	nos hayamos lavado os hayáis lavado se hayan lavado

PLUPERFECT SUBJUNCTIVE

(that) I had washed myself, etc.	me hubiese lavado	nos hubiésemos lavado
	te hubieses lavado	os hubieseis lavado
	se hubiese lavado	se hubiesen lavado

FUTURE PERFECT SUBJUNCTIVE

(if) I shall have washed myself, etc.	me hubiere lavado	nos hubiéremos lavado
	te hubieres lavado	os hubiereis lavado
	se hubiere lavado	se hubieren lavado

CONDITIONAL PERFECT SUBJUNCTIVE

(that) I should have washed myself, etc.	me hubiera lavado	nos hubiéramos lavado
	te hubieras lavado	os hubierais lavado
	se hubiera lavado	se hubieran lavado

INTERROGATIVE FORMS

Questions are formed in Spanish by placing the subject after the verb; *do, does* and *did* are not translated:

do they speak = speak they?	*¿hablan ellos?*
does the car leave = leaves the car?	*¿parte el automóvil?*
would the train arrive?	*¿llegaría el tren?*

In compound tenses formed with *haber*, the subject in questions usually **follows** the past participle:

have your friends come?	*¿han venido sus amigos de Vd.?*
has the man written to them?	*¿les ha escrito el hombre?*
had not the guests dined?	*¿no habían comido los convidados?*
will the workmen have finished?	*¿habrán acabado los obreros?*

(Such constructions as *han sus amigos venido* are not absolutely incorrect, but they are less elegant and never used except for very special literary purposes.

In compound tenses formed with *estar*, the subject in questions may follow or precede the present participle:

are you listening?	*¿está Vd. escuchando?* or *¿está escuchando Vd.?*

NEGATIVE FORMS

Negations are formed in Spanish by putting **no** before the verb; *do, does* and *did* are not translated:

the boy does not work (= works not)	*el muchacho no trabaja*
does he not buy = buys he not?	*¿no compra él?*
they will not write	*(ellos) no escribirán*

In compound tenses, **no** precedes the auxiliary:

the train has not started	*el tren no ha partido*
he cannot understand it	*(el) no puede comprenderlo*

OMISSION OF THE NOMINATIVE PRONOUN

The pronoun which is the subject of a Spanish verb is generally omitted, except in questions:

I have received a letter	*he recibido una carta*
they are downstairs	*están abajo*

It must sometimes be inserted for clearness or emphasis:

I have finished my work; has he finished his?	*he acabado mi trabajo; ¿ha acabado él el suyo?*

Since *Vd.* and *Vds.*, being contractions of *vuestra merced, vuestras mercedes* (*your honour, your honours*), are equivalent to nouns, not pronouns, they therefore cannot be omitted.

TRANSLATION OF 'TO' BEFORE AN INFINITIVE

The second of two verbs coming together must be in the infinitive (the auxiliaries *to be* and *to have* are immediately followed by a past participle, but this rule is otherwise invariable):

we shall let them **speak**	*les dejaremos* **hablar**

1. To before an infinitive is generally translated **de,** unless meaning *in order to*, when it is rendered by **para**:

it is time to start	*es tiempo de partir*
he has waited to see you	*ha esperado para verle*
he said it to prove I had made a mistake	*lo ha dicho para probar que me había equivocado*

2. To is translated by **a** after certain verbs, of which the principal are the following:

andar, to walk	*correr*, to run	*obligar*, to compel
aprender, to learn	*empezar*, to begin	*persuadir*, to persuade
autorizar, to authorize	*enseñar*, to teach	*salir*, to go out
comenzar, to commence	*invitar*, to invite	*venir*, to come
continuar, to continue	*ir*, to go	*volver*, to come back

the girls began to sing	*las muchachas empezaron a cantar*
I will teach him to write	*le enseñaré a escribir*
I am going to get up	*voy a levantarme*

3. To is not translated at all after certain other verbs, the most important of these being listed below:

deber, to owe (must, ought)	*permitir*, to permit
dejar, to allow, to let	*poder*, to be able
desear, to desire, to want	*prometer*, to promise
esperar, to hope	*querer*, to be willing, etc.
hacer, to make	*saber*, to know (how to)
intentar, to intend	*sentir*, to feel (= regret)
mandar, to order, to command	*servirse*, to have the kindness (please)
oir, to hear	*temer*, to fear
parecer, to appear, to seem	*ver*, to see

was he not able to understand you?	*¿no podía comprenderle?*
they want to speak to us	*desean hablarnos*
he promised to show it to me	*prometió mostrármelo*

Irregular Verbs

HOW TO LEARN THEM EASILY

All regular *-ar* verbs are conjugated like *hablar*, all regular *-er* verbs like *deber*, and all regular *ir* verbs like *vivir*. Verbs differing in any respect from these three regular conjugations are called **irregular** verbs. But even the irregularities are subject to certain rules, and when these rules are mastered the irregular verbs present little difficulty.

It is a fatal mistake to suppose (as one might from looking at numerous grammar books) that a verb must be learned from beginning to end of the conjugation because it is irregular in one or two places. If the right plan is adopted, all difficulty disappears. The great secret lies in **thoroughly learning the regular verbs first, and in assuming that the irregular verbs are regular.** They are regular, as a matter of fact, in most parts of the conjugation; the student who assumes this has only to learn the few irregularities instead of the whole conjugation. One might almost call them 'regular' irregular verbs—but see the heading 'irregular' irregularities on page 52. We have split the forthcoming section into two main parts; the first deals with slightly irregular verbs, the second with entirely irregular ones.

However difficult they may be, you should have no trouble whatever in learning them provided that (a) you have studied the regular verbs thoroughly; (b) you assume the irregular verbs to be regular; (c) you follow our original rules for the formation of tenses in irregular verbs. The latter will be found on the next two pages.

FORMATION OF TENSES—IRREGULAR VERBS

1. Except in the present indicative, the terminations are regular throughout the tense. This being so, only the 1st person singular of the other tenses need be learnt. The remainder of the tense (except the present indicative) always takes the same endings as in the regular verbs. (It must be remembered that *dormir* (p. 77), *morir* (p. 81) and the *pedir* and *sentir* groups (pp. 61–63) change the stem vowel in certain parts of the conjugation). The familiar form of the imperative must also be learnt, if the conjugation is to be mastered in its entirety.

2. The stem of the imperfect is always regular.

3. The stems of the future and conditional are always alike.

4. Whenever the stem of the past definite is irregular, the endings of that tense are: **-e, -iste, -o; -imos, -isteis -ieron.**

5. The stem of the imperative (polite form) is always that of the 1st person singular, present indicative.

6. The present subjunctive is the same as the polite form of the imperative.

7. The stem of the remaining tenses of the subjunctive is formed by taking away the final **-ron** from the 3rd person plural of the past definite.

A careful study of these seven rules will simplify the student's work amazingly. When they are properly mastered, he will find that instead of having to learn the conjugation all through, he merely has to learn whatever is irregular in:

(i) The participles
(ii) The present indicative
(iii) The future and past definite stems*

* The 2nd person singular of the imperative of five verbs (*tener*, *hacer*, *poner*, *salir* and *venir*) drops the final *-e*, thus: *ten*, *haz*, *pon*, *sal*, *ven.* But these forms need only be learnt for examination purposes.

Many other tenses are irregular, it is true, but **the remaining irregularities are regular,** so to speak, being subject to the foregoing clearly defined rules, which make the irregularities always identical with those in the above mentioned parts of the verb.

Thus, if the 1st person singular of the present indicative is irregular, the same irregularity invariably occurs in the imperative and the present subjunctive. If the past definite stem is irregular, the remaining tenses of the subjunctive show the same irregularity. If the future is irregular, the conditional is irregular in precisely the same way. The conditional and subjunctive therefore require no learning, even when irregular.

THE RULES APPLIED

Take the exceptionally irregular verb *hacer* (*to do*) as an example of these rules. Instead of learning the full conjugation, you need only note that *done* is *hecho*, *I do* is *hago*, *I did* is *hice* and *I shall do* is *haré*. These four words are an infallible key to the whole conjugation:

(i) As *I do* is *hago*, the polite imperative is *haga*, *hagamos*, *hagan*, and the present subjunctive is *haga*, *hagas*, etc. (rules 5 and 6).

(ii) As *I shall do* is *haré*, the conditional is *haría*, *harías*, etc. (rule 3).

(iii) As *I did* is *hice*, the past definite must be *hice*, *hiciste*, *hizo*; *hicimos*, *hicisteis*, *hicieron* (rule 4).

From *hicieron* we get the rest of the subjunctive, which, by rule 7, must be *hiciese* (imperfect), *hiciere* (future) and *hiciera* (conditional).

The present participle, the imperfect indicative and the remainder of the present indicative, not being mentioned above, are regular; that is, they are formed exactly as in the regular verb *deber*.

'IRREGULAR' IRREGULARITIES

The only irregularities not in accordance with the rules set out on page 50 occur in *dar*, *decir*, *haber*, *ir*, *saber*, *ser* and *ver*. We distinguish these by the title above. All other irregularities may fairly be termed regular, as already shown. The 'irregular' ones follow:

Dar: Although an *-ar* verb, this takes in the past definite the endings of the regular ***-er*** verbs. However, as the stem remains regular, the endings *-e*, *-iste*, *-o*, etc. (rule 4, page 50) are not used.

Haber: This is irregular in the present subjunctive, which is ***haya,*** etc. This is also the polite imperative, which is not much used; for *there is*, *there are*, use *hay* instead of *ha*.

Saber: The polite imperative (and consequently the present subjunctive also) is ***sepa.***

Ver: The imperfect indicative is ***veía***, etc., the ***e*** of the infinitive being retained (not *vía*).

Decir: The 2nd person singular of the imperative is ***di.***

Ir and **ser**: These two are exceptionally irregular, their imperfect (*iba*, *era*), their imperatives (*vaya*, *sea*) and their past definite (*fui*, etc. common to both verbs) being irreducible to rule. The present tense is also quite irregular. All that one can do is learn the irregularities without looking for any reason for them, or any quick way round the problem.

With the exception of *haber* (pages 16–17) and *ser* (pages 20–21) all the above verbs will be found between pages 72–88.

Slightly Irregular Verbs

VERBS CHANGING STRESSED VOWEL OF STEM

A large number of Spanish verbs change the vowel of the stem whenever it takes the stress, but are otherwise perfectly regular. These verbs consist of two groups:

Verbs which change the **e** of the stem to **ie**
Verbs which change the **o** of the stem to **ue**

As the stem never takes the stress except in the present tense, this change of vowel only occurs in the singular and the 3rd person plural of the **imperative**, the **present indicative** and the **present subjunctive**.

As examples of the first group (**e** to **ie**) we give *cerrar* and *perder*, while the second group (**o** to **ue**) is illustrated by *costar* and *mover*.

The lists which follow these examples have been compiled with the greatest care, and are believed to be absolutely complete; at all events, they are considerably more complete than any published before. A few of the verbs included can also be conjugated regularly, and many of them are hardly ever used. There is no need whatever to learn them all by heart; the only really important verbs of this class are given in our grammar 'Spanish in Three Months'.

As these lists are not intended to fulfil the purpose of a dictionary, no attempt has been made to give an exact translation of the words. In many cases this is hardly possible; the English given is merely a hint as to the meaning (to those verbs which have several, only one has been given).

Unless mentioned to the contrary in the footnotes, all of these verbs change the stressed vowel of the stem, no matter in which of their various meanings they are used.

EXAMPLES OF **E** CHANGING TO **IE**

cerrar *to close*

PRESENT INDICATIVE

I close, etc.	cierro	cerramos
	cierras	cerráis
	cierra	cierran

IMPERATIVE

let us close		cerremos
close (thou, ye)	cierra	cerrad
close	cierre Vd.	cierren Vds.

PRESENT SUBJUNCTIVE

(that) I may close,	cierre	cerremos
etc.	cierres	cerréis
	cierre	cierren

All other tenses are regular, conjugated like *hablar.*

perder *to lose*

PRESENT INDICATIVE

I lose, etc.	pierdo	perdemos
	pierdes	perdéis
	pierde	pierden

IMPERATIVE

let us lose		perdamos
lose (thou, ye)	pierde	perded
lose	pierda Vd.	pierdan Vds.

PRESENT SUBJUNCTIVE

(that) I may lose,	pierda	perdamos
etc.	pierdas	perdáis
	pierda	pierdan

All other tenses are regular, conjugated like *deber.*

EXAMPLES OF **O** CHANGING TO **UE**

costar *to cost*

PRESENT INDICATIVE

I cost, etc.	**cue**sto	costamos
	cuestas	costáis
	cuesta	**cue**stan

IMPERATIVE

let us cost		costemos
cost (thou, ye)	**cue**sta	costad
cost	**cue**ste Vd.	**cue**sten Vds.

PRESENT SUBJUNCTIVE

(that) I may cost, etc.	**cue**ste	costemos
	cuestes	costéis
	cueste	**cue**sten

All other tenses are regular, conjugated like *hablar*.

mover *to move*

PRESENT INDICATIVE

I move, etc.	m**ue**vo	movemos
	m**ue**ves	movéis
	m**ue**ve	m**ue**ven

IMPERATIVE

let us move		movamos
move (thou, ye)	m**ue**ve	moved
move	m**ue**va Vd.	m**ue**van Vds.

PRESENT SUBJUNCTIVE

(that) I may move, etc.	m**ue**va	movamos
	m**ue**vas	mováis
	m**ue**va	m**ue**van

All other tenses are regular, conjugated like *deber*.

acertar, *to guess*
acrecentar, *to increase*
adestrar, *to direct*
aferrar,* *to grapple*
alebrarse, *to cower*
alentar, *to encourage*
aliquebrar, *to break a wing*
apacentar, *to pasture*
apernar, *to sieze by the thigh*
apretar, *to press together*
arrendar, *to lease, to rent*
asentar, *to set down*
aserrar, *to saw*
atentar,† *to fumble, grope*
aterrar,‡ *to knock down*
atestar,§ *to cram*
atravesar, *to cross*
aventar, *to fan*
calentar, *to warm*
cegar, *to dazzle*
cerrar, *to shut*
cimentar, *to cement*
comenzar, *to commence*
concertar, *to arrange*
concertarse, *to concert*
confesar, *to confess*
decentar, *to cut into*
denegar, *to deny*
dentar, *to indent*
derrengar, *to strain the hip*
desacertar, *to err*
desaferrar,* *to unfasten*
desalentar, *to discourage*
desapretar, *to loosen*
desarrendarse, *to shake off the bridle*
desasentar, *not to suit*
desasosegar, *to disturb*
desatentar, *to perturb*
desconcertar, *to disconcert*
desdentar, *to draw teeth*
desempedrar, *to unpave*
desencerrar, *to let loose*
desenterrar, *to exhume*
desferrar,* *to free from irons*
desgobernar, *to misgovern*
deshelar, *to thaw*
desherbar, *to remove weeds*
desherrar, *to unshoe horses*
deslendrar, *to clean the hair*
desmelar, *to take honey from a hive*
desmembrar, *to dismember*
desnevar, *to remove snow*
despernar, *to cut off a leg*
despertar, *to awake*
desplegar, *to unfold*
destentar, *to free from temptation*
desterrar, *to exile*
desventar, *to let out the air*
dezmar, *to pay tithes*
emendar, *to amend*

* More often used regularly.
† Regular in the meaning of 'to attempt some one's life': *atento, atentas, atenta; atentamos, atentáis, atentan.*
‡ Regular in the meaning of 'to terrify': *aterro, aterras,* etc.
§ Regular in the meaning of 'to testify': *atesto, atestas,* etc.

emparentar, *to become related by marriage*
empedrar, *to pave*
empezar, *to begin*
encensar, *to perfume*
encerrar, *to shut in*
encomendar, *to recommend*
encubertar, *to cover*
endentar, *to mortise*
enhestar, *to set upright*
enmelar, *to smear with honey*
enmendar, *to correct*
ensangrentar, *to stain with blood*
enterrar, *to bury*
entrepernar, *to cross legs*
escarmentar, *to learn by experience*
estercar, *to manure*
estregar, *to scour*
ferrar, *to point with iron*
fregar, *to rub*
gobernar, *to govern*
hacendar, *to transfer an estate*
helar, *to freeze*
herbar, *to dress skins with plants*
herrar, *to shoe a horse*
incensar, *to perfume*
infernar, *to damn*
invernar, *to pass the winter*
manifestar, *to manifest*
melar, *to deposit honey*
mentar, *to mention*
merendar, *to take afternoon lunch*
negar, *to deny*
nevar, *to snow*
pensar, *to think*
perniquebrar, *to break one's legs*
plegar, *to fold*
quebrar, *to break*
reapretar, *to press again*
reaventar, *to re-winnow*
recalentar, *to re-warm*
recentar, *to leaven*
recomendar, *to recommend*
refregar, *to fray*
regar, *to water*
regimentar, *to maintain discipline, organize*
reherrar, *to re-shoe a horse*
remendar, *to mend*
renegar, *to abjure*
repensar, *to reflect again*
replegar, *to re-double*
requebrar, *to woo*
resegar, *to reap again*
resembrar, *to sow again*
resquebrar, *to split*
retemblar, *to vibrate*
retentar, *to threaten with a relapse*
reventar, *to burst*
salpimentar, *to season with salt and pepper*
sarmentar, *to gather the pruned-off shoots of vines*
segar, *to mow, to cut*
sembrar, *to sow*
sementar, *to scatter seed*
sentar, *to suit*
sentarse, *to sit down*
serrar, *to saw*
sobresembrar, *to sow again*
sorregar, *to change the course of a brook*

sosegar, *to tranquillize*
soterrar, *to bury*
subarrendar, *to sub-let*
temblar, *to tremble*
tentar, *to touch, to try*
transfregar, *to rub*
trasegar, *to pour over*
travesar, *to cross*
tropezar, *to stumble*
ventar, *to blow*

VERBS CONJUGATED LIKE *PERDER*

ascender, *to ascend*
atender, *to await*
cerner,* *to sift*
condescender, *to condescend*
contender, *to condend*
defender, *to defend*
desatender, *to disregard*
descender, *to descend*
desentenderse, *to ignore*
encender, *to light*
entender, *to understand*
extender, *to extend*
heder, *to stink*
hender, *to split, stick into*
perder, *to lose*
reverter, *to overflow*
tender, *to spread out*
trascender, *to transcend*
verter, *to shed*

* *Discernir,* (to discern) was formerly spelt *discerner,* and changes its stressed vowel like *cerner.*

VERBS CONJUGATED LIKE *COSTAR*

abuñolar, *to make egg fritters*
aclocarse, *to hatch eggs*
acordar,* *to agree*
acordarse, *to recollect*
acostar, *to put to bed*
acostarse, *to go to bed*
afollar, *to blow at*
aforar,† *to rent*
afotar, *to rent*
agorar, *to augur*
almorzar, *to breakfast*
alongar, *to lengthen*
amoblar, *to furnish*
amolar, *to grind*
apercollar, *to seize by the collar*
aporcar, to *cover with earth*
aportar,‡ *to land at a port*
apostar,§ *to bet*
aprobar, *to approve*

* Regular in the meaning of 'to tune musical instruments': *acordo, acordas, acorda; acordamos, acordáis, acordan.*

† Regular in the meaning of 'to gauge', 'to appraise': *aforo, aforas,* etc.

‡ Regular in the meaning of 'to bring, supply, provide': *aporto,* etc.

§ Regular in the meaning of 'to station', 'to place': *aposto, apostas,* etc.

asolar, *to raze*
asoldar, *to pay troops*
asonar, *to make sounds accord*
atronar, *to thunder*
avergonzar, *to shame*
avergonzarse, *to be ashamed*
azolar, *to work with an axe*
colar, *to filter*
colgar, *to hang up*
comprobar, *to corroborate*
concordar, *to agree*
consolar, *to console*
consonar, *to harmonize*
contar, *to relate*
costar, *to cost*
degollar, *to behead*
demostrar, *to demonstrate*
denostar, *to revile*
derrocar, *to fling down*
desacordar, *to be in discord*
desaforar, *to encroach on rights*
desamoblar, *to unfurnish*
desaprobar, *to disapprove*
descolgar, *to unhang, take from a hook*
descollar, *to be more prominent than*
desconsolar, *to make disconsolate*
descontar, *to discount*
descornar, *to break off horns*
desencordar, *to unstring*
desengrosar, *to make thinner*
desflocar, *to unravel*
desfogarse, *to get in a passion*
desmajolar, *to uproot vines*
desolar, *to disolate*
desollar, *to flay*
desosar, *to remove bones*
desovar, *to spawn*
despoblar, *to depopulate*
destrocar, *to re-exchange*
desvergonzarse, *to be impudent*
discordar, *to be discordant*
disonar, *to be dissonant*
dolar, *to plane, make smooth*
emporcar, *to soil, stain*
enclocar, *to cluck*
encobar, *to sit on eggs*
encontrar, *to meet, find*
encorar, *to cover with leather*
encorarse, *to cicatrize*
encordar, *to string instruments*
encovar, *to put in a cellar*
engorar, *to addle*
engrosar, *to become stout*
enrodar, *to break on the wheel*
entortar, *to make tortuous*
esforzar, *to encourage*
esforzarse, *to take pains*
follar, *to blow with bellows*
forzar, *to compel*
holgar, *to rest*
hollar, *to trample on*
improbar, *to disapprove*
jugar, *to play*
malsonar, *to sound unpleasant*
moblar, *to furnish*
mostrar, *to show*
poblar, *to populate*
probar, *to prove*
recontar, *to recount*
recordar, *to remind*
recordarse, *to remember*
recostar, *to lean against*
recostarse, *to lie down*

reforzar, *to reinforce*
regoldar, *to belch*
rehollar, *to trample on*
renovar, *to renew*
repoblar, *to re-people*
reprobar, *to reprimand*
rescontrar, *to balance accounts*
resollar, *to breathe hard*
resonar, *to resound*
retostar, *to re-toast*
retronar, *to thunder again*
revolar, *to fly again*
revolcarse, *to wallow*
rodar, *to roll on wheels*
rogar, *to pray, intreat*
sobresolar, *to resole, repave*
solar, *to sole*
soltar, *to loosen*
sonar, *to sound*
sonrodarse, *to stick in the mud (said of a vehicle)*
soñar, *to dream*
tostar, *to toast*
trascolar, *to percolate*
trascordarse, *to misremember*
trasoñar, *to form visionary schemes*
trasvolar, *to fly across*
trocar, *to barter*
tronar, *to thunder*
volar, *to fly*
volcar, *to overturn*

VERBS CONJUGATED LIKE *MOVER*

absolver,* *to absolve*
cocer, *to cook*
condoler, *to condole*
conmover, *to excite emotion*
demoler, *to demolish*
desenvolver, *to unroll*
desmoler, *to disgest*
destorcer, *to untwist*
devolver,* *to restore*
disolver,* *to dissolve*
doler, *to ache*
dolerse, *to grieve*
envolver, *to wrap up*
escocer, *to cause to smart*
llover, *to rain*
moler, *to grind*
morder, *to bite*
mover, *to move*
promover, *to promote*
recocer, *to re-boil*
remorder, *to bite again*
remover, *to remove*
resolver,* *to resolve*
retorcer, *to twist, sprain*
revolver,* *to revolve*
soler, *to be in the habit of*
solver, *to loosen*
torcer, *to twist*
volver*, *to do a thing again, to return*

* These verbs are also irregular in the past participles, which are absuelto, devuelto, disuelto, resuelto, revuelto, vuelto; NOT absolvido, devolvido, disolvido, resolvido, revolvido, volvido.

VERBS CHANGING *UN*STRESSED VOWEL OF STEM

Some verbs (like *perder*—see page 54) change the vowel of the stem whenever it takes the stress, and also change the vowel of the stem, **although unstressed**, in the present participle, the 3rd person singular and plural of the past definite, and throughout the subjunctive (remember that in all verbs the polite imperative is always the same as the present subjunctive). These verbs consist of two groups:

Verbs which change the stressed **e** of the stem to **ie**
Verbs which change the stressed **e** of the stem to **i**

In both groups, the **unstressed e** of the stem is changed to **i** in the above-mentioned parts of the conjugation. Examples, in which this latter change is shown by a bold capital **I**, and lists as before now follow.

sentir *to feel*

PARTICIPLES: *feeling*, s**I**ntiendo *felt*, sentido

PRESENT INDICATIVE

I feel, etc.	s**ie**nto	sentimos
	s**ie**ntes	sentís
	s**ie**nte	s**ie**nten

PAST DEFINITE

I felt, etc.	sentí	sentimos
	sentiste	sentisteis
	s**I**ntió	s**I**ntieron

IMPERATIVE

		let us feel	s**I**ntamos
feel (*thou*)	s**ie**nte	*feel* (*ye*)	sentid
feel (SING.)	s**ie**nta Vd.	*feel* (PLUR.)	s**ie**ntan Vds.
let him feel	que s**ie**nta	*let them feel*	que s**ie**ntan

PRESENT SUBJUNCTIVE

(that) I may feel, etc.	sienta	sIntamos
	sientas	sIntáis
	sienta	sientan

IMPERFECT SUBJUNCTIVE

(that) I felt, etc.	sIntiese	sIntiésemos
	sIntieses	sIntieseis
	sIntiese	sIntiesen

FUTURE SUBJUNCTIVE

(if) I shall feel, etc.	sIntiere	sIntiéremos
	sIntieres	sIntiereis
	sIntiere	sIntieren

CONDITIONAL SUBJUNCTIVE

(that) I should feel, etc.	sIntiera	sIntiéramos
	sIntieras	sIntierais
	sIntiera	sIntieran

pedir *to ask*

PARTICIPLES: *asking*, pIdiendo *asked*, pedido

PRESENT INDICATIVE

I ask, etc.	pido	pedimos
	pides	pedís
	pide	piden

PAST DEFINITE

I asked, etc.	pedí	pedimos
	pediste	pedisteis
	pIdió	pIdieron

IMPERATIVE

		let us ask	pIdamos
ask (thou)	pide	*ask (ye)*	pedid
ask (SING.)	pida Vd.	*ask* (PLUR.)	pidan Vds.
let him ask	que pida	*let them ask*	que pidan

	PRESENT SUBJUNCTIVE	
(*that*) *I may ask, etc.*	p**i**da	p**I**damos
	p**i**das	p**I**dáis
	p**i**da	p**i**dan
	IMPERFECT SUBJUNCTIVE	
(*that*) *I asked, etc.*	p**I**diese	p**I**diésemos
	p**I**dieses	p**I**dieseis
	p**I**diese	p**I**diesen
	FUTURE SUBJUNCTIVE	
(*if*) *I shall ask, etc.*	p**I**diere	p**I**diéremos
	p**I**dieres	p**I**diereis
	p**I**diere	p**I**dieren
	CONDITIONAL SUBJUNCTIVE	
(*that*) *I should ask, etc.*	p**I**diera	p**I**diéramos
	p**I**dieras	p**I**dierais
	p**I**diera	p**I**dieran

VERBS CONJUGATED LIKE *SENTIR*

adherir, *to adhere*
advertir, *to intimate*
arrepentirse, *to repent*
asentir, *to assent*
concernir, *to concern*
conferir, *to confer*
consentir, *to consent*
controvertir, *to controvert*
convertir, *to convert*
deferir, *to pay deference*
desconsentir, *to dissent*
desmentir, *to give the lie to*
diferir, *to postpone*
digerir, *to digest*
discernir, *to discern*
disentir, *to dissent*
divertir, *to amuse*
herir, *to wound*
hervir, *to boil*
inferir, *to infer*
ingerir, *to intrude*
invertir, *to invert*
mentir, *to tell lies*
pervertir, *to pervert*
preferir, *to prefer*
presentir, *to have a presentiment*
proferir, *to utter*
referir, *to refer*
requerir, *to request*
resentirse, *to resent*
sentir, *to feel*
subvertir, *to subvert*
sugerir, *to suggest*
trasferir, *to transfer*
zaherir, *to blame*

VERBS CONJUGATED LIKE *PEDIR*

arrecirse, *to become numbed*
ceñir,* *to gird*
colegir, *to deduce*
comedirse, *to govern onself*
competir, *to compete*
concebir, *to conceive*
conseguir, *to attain*
constreñir,* *to constrain*
corregir, *to correct*
derretir, *to melt*
desceñir,* *to ungird*
descomedirse, *to be rude*
deservir, *to be disobliging*
desleir,* *to dilute*
despedir, *to dismiss*
desperdirse, *to say farewell*
desteñir,* *to lose colour*
elegir, *to elect*
embestir, *to assail*
engreir,* *to make vain*
engreirse, *to become haughty*
envestir, *to clothe*
estreñir,* *to produce astringency*
expedir, *to forward*
freir,* *to fry*
gemir, *to groan*
henchir, *to fill*
heñir,* *to knead*
impedir, *to impede*
investir, *to invest*
medir, *to measure*
pedir, *to ask*
perseguir, *to persecute*
proseguir, *to follow up*
regir, *to rule*
reir,* *to laugh*
rendir, *to yield*
reñir,* *to quarrel*
repetir, *to repeat*
reteñir,* *to re-dye*
revestir, *to re-clothe*
seguir, *to follow*
servir, *to serve*
sonreirse,* *to smile*
teñir,* *to dye*
vestir, *to clothe*

* In verbs conjugated like *pedir*, the unaccented **i** of the termination is **omitted** after "i" or "ñ", thus: laughing, *riendo*; he laughed, *rió*; dyeing, *tiñendo*; they dyed, *tiñeron*; but:—he used to laugh, ***reía***; we used to dye, *te**ñí**amos*, etc.

VERBS ENDING IN -ACER, -ECER, -OCER, -UCIR

Verbs whose infinitive ends in **-acer, -ecer, -ocer,** or **-ucir** change the final **c** of the stem into **zc** before **a** or **o**, but are otherwise perfectly regular (all the tenses of *crecer* not given below are conjugated exactly like *deber*):

crecer *to grow*

PRESENT INDICATIVE

I grow, etc.	cre**zc**o	crecemos
	creces	crecéis
	crece	crecen

IMPERATIVE

let us grow		cre**zc**amos
grow (thou, ye)	crece	creced
grow	cre**zc**a Vd.	cre**zc**an Vds.
let him (them) grow	que cre**zc**a	que cre**zc**an

PRESENT SUBJUNCTIVE

(that) I may grow, etc.	cre**zc**a	cre**zc**amos
	cre**zc**as	cre**zc**áis
	cre**zc**a	cre**zc**an

All the verbs ending in **-acer, -ecer, -ocer** or **-ucir** are conjugated like *crecer*, with the following exceptions:

1. *Yacer* (to lie at rest), and *hacer* (to do) with its compound tenses. For the conjugation of these, see the chapter on ENTIRELY IRREGULAR VERBS.

2. *Mecer* (to rock) and *remecer* (to rock to and fro), which are regular, like *deber*.

3. *Cocer, escocer* and *recocer*, which are conjugated like *mover* (see page 55).

4. The verbs ending in *-ducir*, explained on the next page.

VERBS ENDING IN -DUCIR

These are similar to the preceding verbs ending in *-acer*, *-ecer*, *-ocer*, and *-ucir*, with the addition of a further irregularity in the past definite. This is passed in turn to the three tenses formed from the past definite—the imperfect subjunctive, the future subjunctive and the conditional subjunctive. All verbs ending in *-ducir* are conjugated like *traducir*, any tenses of which not shown below are regular, like *vivir*.

traducir *to translate*

PRESENT INDICATIVE

I translate, etc.	tradu**zco**	traducimos
	traduces	traducís
	traduce	traducen

PAST DEFINITE

I translated, etc.	tradu**je**	tradu**j**imos
	tradu**j**iste	tradu**j**isteis
	tradu**jo**	tradu**je**ron

IMPERATIVE

let us translate		tradu**zc**amos
translate (*thou*, *ye*)	traduce	traducid
translate	tradu**zc**a Vd.	tradu**zc**an Vds.
let him (*them*) *translate*	que tradu**zc**a	que tradu**zc**an

PRESENT SUBJUNCTIVE

(*that*) *I may translate, etc.*	tradu**zc**a	tradu**zc**amos
	tradu**zc**as	tradu**zc**áis
	tradu**zc**a	tradu**zc**an

IMPERFECT SUBJUNCTIVE

(*that*) *I translated, etc.*	tradu**j**ese	tradu**j**ésemos
	tradu**j**eses	tradu**j**eseis
	tradu**j**ese	tradu**j**esen

FUTURE SUBJUNCTIVE

(if) I shall translate, etc.	tradujere	tradujéremos
	tradujeres	tradujereis
	tradujere	tradujeren

CONDITIONAL SUBJUNCTIVE

(that) I should translate, etc.	tradujera	tradujéramos
	tradujeras	tradujerais
	tradujera	tradujeran

VERBS ENDING IN -UIR

Verbs whose infinitive ends in **-uir** add y between the stem and termination in the present indicative, present subjunctive and imperative. This only applies to verbs in which the final **u** of the stem is pronounced, not to such as *distinguir* and *delinquir*— see pages 30–31. *Argüir* is conjugated like *destruir* (see below) because the **u** is pronounced (*arguyo*, *arguyes*, etc.). All the tenses of *destruir* not given below are conjugated exactly like *vivir* (see pages 36–37).

destruir *to destroy*

PRESENT INDICATIVE

I destroy, etc.	destru**yo**	destruimos
	destru**yes**	destruís
	destru**ye**	destru**yen**

IMPERATIVE

let us destroy		destru**yamos**
destroy (thou, ye)	destru**ye**	destruid
destroy	destru**ya** Vd.	destru**yan** Vds.
let him (them) destroy	que destru**ya**	que destru**yan**

PRESENT SUBJUNCTIVE

(that) I may destroy etc.	destru**ya**	destru**yamos**
	destru**yas**	destru**yáis**
	destru**ya**	destru**yan**

IRREGULAR PAST PARTICIPLES

The following verbs are irregular in the **past participle** only:

abrir, *to open*	abierto, *opened*
cubrir, *to cover*	cubierto, *covered*
descubrir, *to discover*	descubierto, *discovered*
encubrir, *to conceal*	encubierto, *concealed*
escribir, *to write*	escrito, *written*
freir, *to fry*	frito,* *fried*
imprimir, *to print*	impreso, *printed*
inscribir, *to inscribe*	inscrito, *or* inscripto,† *inscribed*
prescribir, *to prescribe*	prescrito,* *prescribed*
proscribir, *to proscribe*	proscrito, *or* proscripto,† *proscribed*
proveer, *to provide*	provisto,* *provided*
romper, *to break*	roto,* *broken*

Absolver, *devolver*, *disolver*, *resolver*, *revolver* and *volver*, besides having irregular past participles, change the stressed **o** of the stem to **ue** (see page 53).

* The regular forms, *freido*, *prendido*, *prescribido*, *proveido*, *rompido*, are admissible, but seldom employed.

† The irregular forms *inscripto* and *proscripto* are never used.

ADJECTIVAL PAST PARTICIPLES

Besides their ordinary regular past participle, a great many verbs have what is usually termed an irregular **adjectival past participle.** In deference to custom, we give a list of these, omitting very rarely used and obsolete words; but as the compound tenses of all such verbs—except those mentioned above—are always formed with the regular past participle, such a list is somewhat out of place in a reference book on the verbs, the so-called 'irregular participles' being really adjectives pure and simple.

For instance, *it is dry* is *está enjuto* (adjective); *we have dried it* is *lo hemos enjugado* (past participle, regular). *They are joined* is *están juntos* (adjective); *I have joined them* is *los he juntado* (past participle, regular). To call *junto* an irregular participle of *juntar* is precisely equivalent to saying that such adjectives as *dry*, *open*, *awake*, are irregular past participles of the verbs *to dry*, *to open*, *to wake*.

LIST OF VERBS WITH ADJECTIVAL PAST PARTICIPLES

INFINITIVE	PAST PARTICIPLE (*used in compound tenses*)	VERBAL ADJECTIVE
abstraer, *to abstract*	abstraído	abstracto
aceptar, *to accept*	aceptado	acepto
aficionar, *to inspire affection*	aficionado	afecto
aguzar, *to sharpen, to grind*	aguzado	agudo
ahitar, *to surfeit*	ahitado	ahito
anexar, *to annex*	anexado	anexo
angostar, *to narrow*	angostado	angosto
atender, *to attend*	atendido	atento
bendecir, *to bless*	bendecido	bendito
bienquerer, *to esteem*	bienquerido	bienquisto
circuncidar, *to circumcise*	circuncidado	circunciso
compajinar, *to join*	compajinado	compacto
compeler, *to compel*	compelido	compulso
completar, *to complete*	completado	completo
comprimir, *to compress*	comprimido	compreso
concluir, *to conclude*	concluido	concluso
confesar, *to confess*	confesado	confeso
confundir, *to confound*	confundido	confuso
contentar, *to content*	contentado	contento
contundir, *to bruise*	contundido	contuso
convencer, *to convince*	convencido	convicto
convulsarse, *to become convulsed*	convulsado	convulso
corregir, *to correct*	corregido	correcto
corromper, *to corrupt*	corrompido	corrupto
corvar, *to crook, to bend*	corvado	corvo
cultivar, *to cultivate*	cultivado	culto

INFINITIVE	PAST PARTICIPLE (*used in compound tenses*)	VERBAL ADJECTIVE
densar, *to condense*	densado	denso
descalzar, *to take off the shoes*	descalzado	descalzo
desertar, *to desert*	desertado	desierto
desnudar, *to denude*	desnudado	desnudo
despertar, *to awake*	despertado	despierto
difundir, *to diffuse*	difundido	difuso
dirijir, *to direct*	dirijido	directo
dispersar, *to disperse*	dispersado	disperso
distinguir, *to distinguish*	distinguido	distinto
elejir, *to elect*	elejido	electo
enjugar, *to dry*	enjugado	enjuto
erijir, *to erect*	erijido	erecto
espesar, *to thicken*	espesado	espeso
estrechar, *to narrow*	estrechado	estrecho
estreñir, *to stop*	estreñido	estricto
exceptuar, *to except*	exceptuado	excepto
excluir, *to exclude*	excluido	excluso
eximir, *to exempt*	eximido	exento
expeler, *to expel*	expelido	expulso
experimentar, *to try*	experimentado	experto
expresar, *to express*	expresado	expreso
extender, *to extend*	extendido	extenso
extinguir, *to extinguish*	extinguido	extinto
extraer, *to draw out*	extraído	extracto
falsear, *to falsify*	falseado	falso
faltar, *to want*	faltado	falto
favorecer, *to favour*	favorecido	favorito
fijar, *to fix*	fijado	fijo
hartar, *to satiate*	hartado	harto
incluir, *to include*	incluido	incluso
incurrir, *to incur*	incurrido	incurso
infartar, *to obstruct*	infartado	infarto
infectar, *to infect*	infectado	infecto
infundir, *to pour in*	infundido	infuso
injerir, *to graft*	injerido	injerto
injertar, *to graft*	injertado	injerto
insertar, *to insert*	insertado	inserto
intrusarse, *to intrude*	intrusado	intruso
invertir, *to invert*	invertido	inverso

INFINITIVE	PAST PARTICIPLE (*used in compound tenses*)	VERBAL ADJECTIVE
juntar, *to join*	juntado	junto
limpiar, *to clean*	limpiado	limpio
maldecir, *to curse*	maldecido	maldito
malquistar, *to excite disputes*	malquistado	malquisto
mancar, *to be wanting*	mancado	manco
manifestar, *to manifest*	manifestado	manifiesto
marchitar, *to wither*	marchitado	marchito
nacer, *to be born*	nacido	nato
ocultar, *to hide*	ocultado	oculto
perfeccionar, *to perfect*	perfeccionado	perfecto
pervertir, *to pervert*	pervertido	perverso
presumir, *to presume*	presumido	presunto
producir, *to produce*	producido	producto
profesar, *to profess*	profesado	profeso
propender, *to lean towards*	propendido	propenso
ranciarse, *to become rancid*	ranciado	rancio
recluir, *to seclude*	recluido	recluso
reflejar, *to reverberate*	reflejado	reflejo
repletar, *to fill*	repletado	repleto
restrinjir, *to restrain*	restrinjido	restricto
salpresar, *to pickle*	salpresado	salpreso
salvar, *to save*	salvado	salvo
secar, *to dry*	secado	seco
sepultar, *to bury*	sepultado	sepulto
situar, *to situate, to place*	situado	sito
soltar, *to let loose*	soltado	suelto
sujetar, *to subject*	sujetado	sujeto
surjir, *to come forth, to rise*	surjido	surto
suspender, *to suspend*	suspendido	suspenso
sustituir, *to substitute*	sustituido	sustituto
teñir, *to dye*	teñido	tinto
torcer, *to twist*	torcido	tuerto
vaciar, *to empty, to evacuate*	vaciado	vacío
yuntar, *to put oxen in harness*	yuntado	yunto

Entirely Irregular Verbs

The irregular verbs on pages 72–88 cannot be classified into groups. The list is for reference only; before studying it you should have read and understood our rules on the formation of tenses (pages 50–51). From these it will be seen that the **conditional** and the four **subjunctive** tenses need never be learnt —the **imperative** and **imperfect** indicative, hardly ever.

As the **endings are always regular except in the present indicative**, only the 1st person singular of the remaining tenses need be learnt. Unless otherwise stated, the compound tenses are conjugated like those from which they are derived: i.e. *suponer* is like *poner*, *convenir* is like *venir*, and so on. All irregularities are shown in **bold** type.

adquirir *to acquire*

PARTICIPLES: *acquiring* adquiriendo; *acquired* adquirido

PRESENT INDICATIVE: *I acquire, etc.* adqu**ie**ro, adqu**ie**res, adqu**ie**re; adquirimos, adquirís, adqu**ie**ren

IMPERFECT: *I used to acquire, etc.* adquiría, adquirías, etc.

PAST DEFINITE: *I acquired, etc.* adquirí, adquiriste, etc.

FUTURE: *I shall acquire, etc.* adquiriré, adquirirás, etc.

CONDITIONAL: *I should acquire, etc.* adquiriría, etc.

IMPERATIVE: *acquire* adqu**ie**re, adqu**ie**ra Vd.; adquirid, adqu**ie**ran Vds.; *let us acquire* adquiramos

PRESENT SUBJ.: adqu**ie**ra, adqu**ie**ras, adqu**ie**ra; adquiramos, adquiráis, adqu**ie**ran

IMPERFECT SUBJ.: adquiriese, adquirieses, etc.

FUTURE SUBJ.: adquiriere, adquirieres, etc.

CONDITIONAL SUBJ.: adquiriera, adquirieras, etc.

andar *to walk*

PARTICIPLES: walking, andando; *walked*, andado.

PRESENT INDICATIVE: *I walk, etc.*, ando, andas, anda; andamos, andáis, andan.

IMPERFECT: *I used to walk, etc.*, andaba, andabas, etc.

PAST DEFINITE: *I walked, etc.*, and**uve**, and**uvi**ste, and**uvo**; and**uvi**mos, and**uvi**steis, and**uvie**ron.

FUTURE: *I shall walk, etc.*, andaré, andarás, andará, etc.

CONDITIONAL: *I should walk, etc.*, andaría, andarías, etc.

IMPERATIVE: *walk*, anda, ande Vd.; andad, anden Vds.; *let us walk*, andemos.

PRESENT SUBJ.: ande, andes, ande; andemos, etc.

IMPERFECT SUBJ.: and**uvie**se, and**uvie**ses, etc.

FUTURE SUBJ.: and**uvie**re, and**uvie**res, etc.

CONDITIONAL SUBJ.: and**uvie**ra, and**uvie**ras, etc.

asir *to grasp*

PARTICIPLES: *grasping*, asiendo; *grasped*, asido.

PRESENT INDICATIVE: *I grasp, etc.*, as**g**o, ases, ase; asimos, asís, asen.

IMPERFECT: *I used to grasp, etc.*, asía, asías, asía, etc.

PAST DEFINITE: *I grasped, etc.*, así, asiste, asió; asimos, etc.

FUTURE: *I shall grasp, etc.*, asiré, asirás, asirá; asiremos, etc.

CONDITIONAL: *I should grasp, etc.*, asiría, asirías, etc.

IMPERATIVE: *grasp*, ase, as**g**a Vd.; asid, as**g**an Vds.; *let us grasp*, as**g**amos.

PRESENT SUBJ.: as**g**a, as**g**as, as**g**a; as**g**amos, etc.

IMPERFECT SUBJ.: asiese, asieses, asiese, etc.

FUTURE SUBJ.: asiere, asieres, asiere, etc.

CONDITIONAL SUBJ.: asiera, asieras, asiera, etc.

caber *to be able to be contained**

PARTICLES: cabiendo, cabido.

PRESENT INDICATIVE: **quep**o, cabes, cabe; cabemos, cabéis, caben.

IMPERFECT: cabía, cabías, cabía, cabíamos, cabíais, cabían.

PAST DEFINITE,: **cupe**, **cup**iste, **cupo**; **cup**imos, **cup**isteis, **cupie**ron.

FUTURE: cabré, cabrás, cabrá; cabremos, cabréis, cabrán.

CONDITIONAL: cabría, cabrías, cabría; cabríamos, etc.

IMPERATIVE: cabe, **quep**a; cabed, **quep**an; **quep**amos.

PRESENT SUBJ.: **quep**a, **quep**as, **quep**a, etc.

IMPERFECT SUBJ.: **cup**iese, **cup**ieses, **cup**iese, etc.

FUTURE SUBJ.: **cup**iere, **cup**ieres, **cup**iere, etc.

CONDITIONAL SUBJ.: **cup**iera, **cup**ieras, **cup**iera, etc.

* There is no corresponding English for this difficult verb. The following examples will show how it is usually employed.

This room used to hold all his furniture = All his furniture was able to be contained in this room, *Todos sus muebles* **cabían** *en este cuarto*; There is room for me here = I am able to be contained here, **Quepo** *aquí*.

caer *to fall*

PARTICIPLES: *falling*, cayendo; *fallen*, caído

PRESENT INDICATIVE: *I fall, etc.*, ca**ig**o, caes, cae; caemos, caéis, caen.

IMPERFECT: *I used to fall, etc.*, caía, caías, caía, etc.

PAST DEFINITE: *I fell, etc.*, caí, caíste, ca**y**o; caímos, caísteis, ca**y**eron.

FUTURE: *I shall fall, etc.*, caeré, caerás, caerá; caeremos, etc.

CONDITIONAL: *I should fall, etc.*, caería, caerías, etc.

IMPERATIVE: *fall*, cae, ca**ig**a Vd.; caed, ca**ig**an Vds.; *let us fall*, ca**ig**amos.

PRESENT SUBJ.: ca**ig**a, ca**ig**as, ca**ig**a, etc.

IMPERFECT SUBJ.: ca**y**ese, etc.

FUTURE SUBJ.: ca**y**ere, etc.

CONDITIONAL SUBJ.: ca**y**era, etc.

dar *to give*

PARTICIPLES: *giving*, dando; *given*, dado.

PRESENT INDICATIVE: *I give, etc.*, d**oy**, das, da; damos, dais, dan.

IMPERFECT: *I used to give, etc.*, daba, dabas, daba, etc.

PAST DEFINITE: *I gave etc.*, d**i**, d**iste**, d**io,** d**i**mos, d**i**steis, d**ie**ron.

FUTURE: *I shall give, etc.*, daré, darás, dará; daremos, etc.

CONDITIONAL: *I should give, etc.*, daría, darías, daría, etc.

IMPERATIVE: *give*, da, dé Vd.; dad, den Vds.; *let us give*, demos.

PRESENT SUBJ.: **dé**, des, **dé**; demos, deis, den.

IMPERFECT SUBJ: **die**se, **die**ses, **die**se, etc.

FUTURE SUBJ.: **die**re, **die**res, **die**re, etc.

CONDITIONAL SUBJ.: **die**ra, **die**ras, **die**ra, etc.

NOTE: *Dar*, although ending in **-ar**, takes in the past definite the terminations of the **-er** verbs. The same irregularity therefore occurs in the three subjunctive tenses formed from the past definite.

decir *to say, to tell*

PARTICIPLES: *saying, telling*, diciendo; *said, told*, **dicho**.

PRESENT INDICATIVE: *I say, etc.*, **digo**, **dices**, **dice**, decimos, decís, **dicen**.

IMPERFECT: *I used to say, etc.*, decía, decías, decía, etc.

PAST DEFINITE: *I said, etc.*, **dije**, **dij**iste, **dijo**; **dij**imos, **dij**isteis, **dij**eron.

FUTURE: *I shall say, etc.*, **dir**é, **dir**ás, **dir**á; **dir**emos, etc.

CONDITIONAL: *I should say, etc.*, **dir**ía, **dir**ías, **dir**ía, etc.

IMPERATIVE: *say, tell*, **di**, **dig**a Vd.; decid, **dig**an Vds.; *let us say, let us tell*, **dig**amos.

PRESENT SUBJ.: **dig**a, **dig**as, **dig**a, etc.

IMPERFECT SUBJ.: **dij**ese, **dij**eses, **dij**ese, etc.

FUTURE SUBJ.: **dij**ere, **dij**eres, **dij**ere, etc.

CONDITIONAL SUBJ.: **dij**era, **dij**eras, **dij**era, etc.

NOTE: All the compounds of *decir* (*contradecir*, to contradict; *predecir*, to predict, etc.) take **-dice** instead of **-di** in the singular familiar form of the imperative, thus: *contra***dice**. The past participle and the future stem of the compounds of *decir* are regular.

desosar *to remove bones*

PRESENT INDICATIVE: des**hue**so, des**hue**sas, des**hue**sa, desosamos, desosáis, des**hue**san.

IMPERATIVE: desosa, des**hue**se Vd.; desosad, des**hue**sen Vds.; desosemos.

PRESENT SUBJ.: des**hue**se, des**hue**ses, etc.

NOTE: This verb is conjugated like *costar* (see page 55), except that the stressed **o** of the stem is changed to **hue** instead of to **ue**. All the tenses not given above are quite regular.

dormir *to sleep*

PARTICIPLES: *sleeping*, d**u**rmiendo; *slept*, dormido.

PRESENT INDICATIVE: *I sleep, etc.*, d**ue**rmo, d**ue**rmes, d**ue**rme; dormimos, dormís, d**ue**rmen.

IMPERFECT: *I used to sleep, etc.*, dormía, dormías, etc.

PAST DEFINITE: *I slept, etc.*, dormí, dormiste, d**u**rmió; dormimos, dormisteis, d**u**rmieron.

FUTURE: *I shall sleep, etc.*, dormiré, dormirás, etc.

CONDITIONAL: *I should sleep, etc.*, dormiría, dormirías, etc.

IMPERATIVE: *sleep*, d**ue**rme, d**ue**rma Vd.; dormid, d**ue**rman Vds.; *let us sleep*, d**u**rmamos.

PRESENT SUBJ.: d**ue**rma, d**ue**rmas, d**ue**rma; d**u**rmamos, d**u**rmáis, d**ue**rman.

IMPERFECT SUBJ.: d**u**rmiese, d**u**rmieses, etc.

FUTURE SUBJ.: d**u**rmiere, d**u**rmieres, etc.

CONDITIONAL SUBJ.: d**u**rmiera, d**u**rmieras, etc.

NOTE: The irregularities of *dormir* correspond to those of the *sentir* group, as, besides changing the **o** of the stem to **ue** when stressed, this verb changes the unstressed **o** to **u** exactly where *sentir* changes the unstressed **e** to **i**. *Morir* is conjugated like *dormir*, except that its past participle is irregular.

erguir *to stand erect*

PARTICIPLES: **irguiendo**, erguido

PRESENT INDICATIVE: **yergo** *or* **irgo**, **yergues** *or* **irgues**, **yergue** *or* **irgue**; erguimos, erguís, **yerguen** *or* **irguen**.

IMPERFECT: erguía, erguías, erguía; erguíamos, etc.

PAST DEFINITE: erguí, erguiste, **irguió**; erguimos, erguisteis, **irguieron**.

FUTURE: erguiré, erguirás, erguirá; erguiremos, etc.

CONDITIONAL: erguiría, erguirías, erguiría, etc.

IMPERATIVE: **yergue** *or* **irgue**, **yerga** Vd. *or* **irga** Vd.; erguid, **yergan** Vds. *or* **irgan** Vds.; **yergamos** *or* **irgamos**.

PRESENT SUBJ.: **yerga** *or* **irga**, etc.

IMPERFECT SUBJ.: **irguiese**, **irguieses**, etc.

FUTURE SUBJ.: **irguiere**, **irguieres**, etc.

CONDITIONAL SUBJ.: **irguiera**, **irguieras**, etc.

NOTE: **hi-** is sometimes substituted for **y-** in conjugating this verb, thus: *hiergo, hierga*, etc.; but the Spanish Academy does not accept this form as correct. As **y** is equivalent to **i** the first form of conjugation given above corresponds to that of the *sentir* group (page 61), and the second form to the *pedir* group (page 62).

errar *to err*

PARTICIPLES: *erring*, errando; *erred*, errado.

PRESENT INDICATIVE: *I err, etc.*, **yerro**, **yerras**, **yerra**; erramos, erráis, **yerran**.

IMPERFECT: *I used to err, etc.*, erraba, errabas, etc.

PAST DEFINITE: *I erred, etc.*, erré, erraste, erró, etc.

FUTURE: *I shall err, etc.*, erraré, errarás, errará, etc.

CONDITIONAL: *I should err, etc.*, erraría, errarías, etc.

IMPERATIVE: *err*, yerra, yerre Vd.; errad, yerren Vds.; *let us err*, erremos.

PRESENT SUBJ.: yerre, yerres, yerre; erremos, erréis, yerren.

IMPERFECT SUBJ: errase, errases, errase, etc.

FUTURE SUBJ.: errare, errares, errare, etc.

CONDITIONAL SUBJ.: errara, erraras, errara, etc.

estar *to be*; **haber** *to have*

(These verbs are fully conjugated on pages 22–23, 16–17)

hacer *to do, to make*

PARTICIPLES: *doing, making*, haciendo; *done, made*, h**echo.**

PRESENT INDICATIVE: *I do, I make, etc.*, ha**g**o, haces, hace; hacemos, hacéis, hacen.

IMPERFECT: *I used to do* or *make, etc.*, hacía, hacías, etc.

PAST DEFINITE: *I did, I made, etc.*, h**ice**, h**i**ciste, h**izo**; h**i**cimos, h**i**cisteis, h**i**cieron.

FUTURE: *I shall do, make, etc.*, h**aré**, h**arás**, h**ará**, etc.

CONDITIONAL: *I should do, make, etc.*, h**ar**ía, h**ar**ías, etc.

IMPERATIVE: *do, make*, ha**z**, ha**g**a Vd.; haced, ha**g**an, Vds.; *let us do* or *make*, ha**g**amos.

PRESENT SUBJ.: ha**g**a, ha**g**as, ha**g**a; ha**g**amos, etc.

IMPERFECT SUBJ.: h**i**ciese, h**i**cieses, h**i**ciese, etc.

FUTURE SUBJ.: h**i**ciere, h**i**cieres, h**i**ciere, etc.

CONDITIONAL SUBJ.: h**i**ciera, h**i**cieras, h**i**ciera, etc.

NOTE: All the compounds of *hacer*, such as *contrahacer* (to counterfeit), are conjugated like *hacer*, as are also the two verbs *satisfacer* (to satisfy), and the rarely used *rarefacer* (to rarefy); but the imperative singular of *satisfacer* is sometimes made regular (*satisface* or *satisfaz*).

inquirir *to enquire*

(This verb is conjugated like *adquirir*—see page 72)

ir *to go*

PARTICIPLES: *going*, **y**endo; *gone*, ido.

PRESENT INDICATIVE: *I go, etc.*, **voy**, **vas**, **va**; **va**mos, **va**is, **va**n.

IMPERFECT: *I used to go, etc.*, i**b**a, i**b**as, i**b**a; í**b**amos, i**b**ais, i**ba**n.

PAST DEFINITE: *I went, etc.*, **fui**, **fu**iste, **fue**; **fu**imos, **fu**isteis, **fu**eron.

FUTURE: *I shall go, etc.*, iré, irás, irá; iremos, iréis, irán.

CONDITIONAL: *I should go, etc.*, iría, irías, iría, etc.

IMPERATIVE: *go*, **v**e, **vaya** Vd.; id, **vay**an Vds.; *let us go*, **va**mos (*or* **vaya**mos).

PRESENT SUBJ.: **vay**a, **vay**as, **vay**a, etc.

IMPERFECT SUBJ.: **fu**ese, etc.

FUTURE SUBJ.: **fu**ere, etc.

CONDITIONAL SUBJ.: **fu**era, etc.

NOTE: *Irse* (to go away) has of course the same irregularities. For conjugation of a verb used reflexively, see pages 43 to 46.

The past definite of *ir* is identical with that of *ser* (see page 20).

jugar *to play*

PARTICIPLES: *playing*, jugando; *played*, jugado.

PRESENT INDICATIVE: *I play, etc.*, **jue**go, **jue**gas, **jue**ga; jugamos, jugáis, **jue**gan.

IMPERATIVE: *play*, **jue**ga, **jue**gue Vd.; jugad, **jue**guen Vds.; *let us play*, juguemos.

PRESENT SUBJ.: **jue**gue, **jue**gues, **jue**gue; juguemos, juguéis, **jue**guen.

NOTE: This verb changes the stressed **u** of the stem to **ue**, and is therefore included in the group conjugated like *costar* (see page 55, and remarks on page 30). All the tenses not given here are perfectly regular.

morir *to die*

PARTICIPLES: *dying*, m**u**riendo; *died*, m**uerto**.

PRESENT INDICATIVE: *I die, etc.*, m**ue**ro, m**ue**res, m**ue**re; morimos, morís, m**ue**ren.

IMPERFECT: *I was dying, etc.*, moría, morías, moría, etc.

PAST DEFINITE: *I died, etc.*, morí, moriste, m**u**rió; morimos, moristeis, m**u**rieron.

FUTURE: *I shall die, etc.*, moriré, morirás, morirá, etc.

CONDITIONAL: *I should die, etc.*, moriría, morirías, etc.

IMPERATIVE: *die*, m**ue**re, m**ue**ra Vd.; morid, m**ue**ran Vds.; *let us die*, m**u**ramos.

PRESENT SUBJ.: m**ue**ra, m**ue**ras, m**ue**ra, m**u**ramos, m**u**ráis, m**ue**ran.

IMPERFECT SUBJ: m**u**riese, m**u**rieses, m**u**riese, etc.

FUTURE SUBJ.: m**u**riere, m**u**rieres, m**u**riere, etc.

CONDITIONAL SUBJ.: m**u**riera, m**u**rieras, m**u**riera, etc.

NOTE: Except the past participle, *morir* is conjugated exactly like *dormir.*

oir *to hear*

PARTICIPLES: *hearing*, o**y**endo; *heard*, oído.

PRESENT INDICATIVE: *I hear, etc.*, o**ig**o, o**y**es, o**y**e; oímos, oís, o**y**en.

IMPERFECT: *I used to hear, etc.*, oía, oías, oía; oíamos, etc.

PAST DEFINITE: *I heard, etc.*, oí, oíste, **oyó**; oímos, oísteis, **oyeron**.

FUTURE: *I shall hear, etc.*, oiré, oirás, oirá; oiremos, etc.

CONDITIONAL: *I should hear, etc.*, oiría, oirías, oiría, etc.

IMPERATIVE: *hear*, **oye**, **oiga** Vd.; oíd, **oigan** Vds.; *let us hear*, **oigamos**.

PRESENT SUBJ.: **oiga, oigas, oiga; oigamos, etc.**

IMPERFECT SUBJ.: **oyese, oyeses, oyese, etc.**

FUTURE SUBJ.: **oyere, oyeres, oyere, etc.**

CONDITIONAL SUBJ.: **oyera, oyeras, oyera, etc.**

oler *to smell*

PARTICIPLES: *smelling*, oliendo; *smelt*, olido,

PRESENT INDICATIVE: *I smell, etc.*, **hue**lo, **hue**les, **hue**le; olemos, oléis, **hue**len.

IMPERATIVE: *smell*, **hue**le, **hue**la Vd.; oled, **hue**lan, Vds.; *let us smell*, olamos.

PRESENT SUBJ.: **hue**la, **hue**las, **hue**la; olamos, oláis, **hue**lan.

NOTE: This verb is conjugated like *mover* (see page 55), except that—as in *desosar*—the stressed **o** of the stem is changed to **hue-** instead of to **-ue-**. All the tenses not given above are quite regular.

poder *to be able to*

PARTICIPLES: *being able to*, p**u**diendo; *been able to*, podido.

PRESENT INDICATIVE: *I am able to* (*can*), *etc.*, p**ue**do, p**ue**des, p**ue**de; podemos, podéis, p**ue**den.

IMPERFECT: *I used to be able to* (*could*), *etc.*, podía, etc.

PAST DEFINITE: *I was able to, etc.*, **pude**, **pudiste**, **pudo**; **pudimos**, **pudisteis**, **pudieron**.

FUTURE: *I shall be able to, etc.*, po**dr**é, po**dr**ás, etc.

CONDITIONAL: *I should be able to, etc.*, po**dr**ía, etc.

PRESENT SUBJ.: p**ue**da, p**ue**das, p**ue**da, etc.

IMPERFECT SUBJ.: p**u**diese p**u**dieses, etc.

FUTURE SUBJ.: p**u**diere, p**u**dieres, etc.

CONDITIONAL SUBJ.: p**u**diera, p**u**dieras, etc.

podrir (or **pudrir**) *to rot*

PARTICIPLES: *rotting*, p**u**driendo; *rotted*, podrido

PRESENT INDICATIVE: *I rot, etc.*, p**u**dro, p**u**dres, p**u**dre; podrimos, podrís, p**u**dren.

IMPERFECT: *I used to rot, etc.*, podría, podrías, etc.

PAST DEFINITE: *I rotted, etc.*, podrí, podriste, p**u**drió; podrimos, podristeis, p**u**drieron.

FUTURE: *I shall rot, etc.*, podriré, podrirás, podrirá, etc.

CONDITIONAL: *I should rot, etc.*, podriría, podrirías, etc.

IMPERATIVE: *rot*, p**u**dre, p**u**dra Vd.; podrid, p**u**dran Vds.; *let us rot*, p**u**dramos.

PRESENT SUBJ.: p**u**dra, p**u**dras, p**u**dra; p**u**dramos. p**u**dráis, p**u**dran.

IMPERFECT SUBJ.: p**u**driese, etc.

FUTURE SUBJ.: p**u**driere, etc.

CONDITIONAL SUBJ.: p**u**driera, etc.

NOTE: The **u**'s printed above in thick type only constitute irregularities if the infinitive is spelt *podrir*. But with the exception of the past participle, which is always *podrido*, **u** may be substituted for **o** throughout the conjugation, thus: past definite *pudrí, pudriste;* future *pudriré*; conditional *pudriría*, etc., etc. The result of this substitution is a verb (*pudrir*) absolutely regular in every number, person, mood and tense, except in the past participle, where *podrido* is the only admissible form. This simple plan, which is recommended by the Spanish Academy, has the additional advantage of making the imperfect tense of this verb distinct from the conditional of *poder*.

poner *to put*

PARTICIPLES: *putting*, poniendo; *put*, p**uesto**.

PRESENT INDICATIVE: *I put, etc.*, pon**g**o, pones, pone; ponemos, ponéis, ponen.

IMPERFECT: *I used to put, etc.*, ponía, ponías, ponía, etc.

PAST DEFINITE: *I put, etc.*, p**use**, p**us**iste, p**uso**; p**us**imos, p**us**isteis, p**us**ieron.

FUTURE: *I shall put, etc.*, pon**d**ré, pon**d**rás, pon**d**rá, etc.

CONDITIONAL: *I should put, etc.*, pon**d**ría, pon**d**rías, etc.

IMPERATIVE: *put*, **pon**, ponga Vd.; poned, pon**g**an, Vds.; *let us put*, pon**g**amos.

PRESENT SUBJ.; pon**g**a, pon**g**as, pon**g**a, etc.

IMPERFECT SUBJ.: p**us**iese, p**us**ieses, etc.

FUTURE: SUBJ.: p**us**iere, p**us**ieres, etc.

CONDITIONAL SUBJ.: p**us**iera, p**us**ieras, etc.

querer *to like to, be willing to, wish to, want to*

PARTICIPLES: *wishing to*, queriendo; *wished to*, querido.

PRESENT INDICATIVE: *I wish, etc.*, qu**ie**ro, qu**ie**res, qu**ie**re; queremos, queréis, qu**ie**ren.

IMPERFECT: *I used to wish, etc.*, quería, querías, etc.

PAST DEFINITE: *I wished, etc.*, qu**ise**, qu**is**iste, qu**iso**; qu**is**imos, qu**is**isteis, qu**is**ieron.

FUTURE: *I shall wish, etc.*, que**rr**é, que**rr**ás, etc.

CONDITIONAL: *I should wish, etc.*, que**rr**ía, querrías, etc.

IMPERATIVE: *wish*, qu**ie**re, qu**ie**ra Vd.; quered, qu**ie**ran Vds.; *let us wish*, queramos.

PRESENT SUBJ.: qu**ie**ra, qu**ie**ras, qu**ie**ra; queramos, queráis, qu**ie**ran.

IMPERFECT SUBJ.: qu**is**iese, qu**is**ieses, etc.

FUTURE SUBJ.: qu**is**iere, qu**is**ieres, etc.

CONDITIONAL SUBJ.: qu**is**iera, qu**is**ieras, etc.

saber *to know*

PARTICIPLES: *knowing*, sabiendo; *known*, sabido.

PRESENT INDICATIVE: *I know, etc.*, s**é**, sabes, sabe; sabemos, sabéis, saben.

IMPERFECT: *I used to know, etc.*, sabía, sabías, sabía, etc.

PAST DEFINITE: *I knew, etc.*, s**upe**, s**up**iste, s**upo**; s**up**imos, s**up**isteis, s**up**ieron.

FUTURE: *I shall know, etc.*, sa**b**r**é**, sa**br**ás, sa**br**á, etc.

CONDITIONAL: *I should know, etc.*, sa**br**ía, sa**br**ías, etc.

IMPERATIVE: *know*, sabe, s**ep**a Vd.; sabed, s**ep**an Vds.; *let us know*, s**ep**amos.

PRESENT SUBJ.: s**ep**a, s**ep**as, s**ep**a; s**ep**amos, etc.

IMPERFECT SUBJ.: s**up**iese, s**up**ieses, etc.

FUTURE SUBJ.: s**up**iere, s**up**ieres, etc.

CONDITIONAL SUBJ.: s**up**iera, s**up**ieras, etc.

salir *to go out*

PARTICIPLES: *going out*, saliendo; *gone out*, salido.

PRESENT INDICATIVE: *I go out, etc.*, sal**g**o, sales, sale; salimos, salís, salen.

IMPERFECT: *I used to go out, etc.*, salía, salías, salía, etc.

PAST DEFINITE: *I went out, etc.*, salí, saliste, salió; salimos salisteis, salieron.

FUTURE: *I shall go out, etc.*, sal**d**ré, sal**d**rás sal**d**rá, etc.

CONDITIONAL: *I should go out, etc.*, sal**d**ría, sal**d**rías, etc.

IMPERATIVE: *go out*, **sal**, sal**g**a Vd.; salid, sal**g**an Vds.; *let us go out*, sal**g**amos.

PRESENT SUBJ.: sal**g**a, sal**g**as, sal**g**a, etc.

IMPERFECT SUBJ.: saliese, etc.

FUTURE SUBJ.: saliere, etc.

CONDITIONAL SUBJ.: saliera, etc.

satisfacer *to satisfy*

(see footnote to *hacer*, page 79)

ser *to be*; **tener** *to have*

(These verbs are fully conjugated on pages 18–21)

traer *to bring*

PARTICIPLES: *bringing*, tra**y**endo; *brought*, traído

PRESENT INDICATIVE: *I bring, etc.*, tra**ig**o, traes, trae; traemos, traéis, traen.

IMPERFECT: *I used to bring, etc.*, traía, traías, traía, etc.

PAST DEFINITE: *I brought, etc.*, tra**je**, tra**j**iste, tra**jo**; tra**j**imos, tra**j**isteis, tra**j**eron.

FUTURE: *I shall bring, etc.*, traeré, traerás, traerá, etc.

CONDITIONAL: *I should bring, etc.*, traería, traerías, etc.

IMPERATIVE: *bring*, trae, **traiga** Vd.; traed, **traigan** Vds.; *let us bring*, **traigamos**.

PRESENT SUBJ.: **traiga, traigas, traiga**, etc.

IMPERFECT SUBJ.: **trajese**, etc.

FUTURE SUBJ.: **trajere**, etc.

CONDITIONAL SUBJ.: **trajera**, etc.

valer *to be worth*

PARTICIPLES: *being worth*, valiendo; *been worth*, valido.

PRESENT INDICATIVE: *I am worth, etc.*, **valgo**, vales, vale; valemos, valéis, valen.

IMPERFECT: *I used to be worth, etc.*, valía, valías, etc.

PAST DEFINITE: *I was worth, etc.*, valí, valiste, valió; valimos, valisteis, valieron.

FUTURE: *I shall be worth, etc.*, **valdré, valdrás, valdrá**, etc.

CONDITIONAL: *I should be worth, etc.*, **valdría, valdrías**, etc.

IMPERATIVE: *be worth*, vale, **valga** Vd.; valed, **valgan** Vds.; *let us be worth*, **valgamos**.

PRESENT SUBJ.: **valga, valgas, valga**, etc.

IMPERFECT SUBJ.: valiese, valieses, valiese, etc.

FUTURE SUBJ.: valiere, valieres, valiere, etc.

CONDITIONAL SUBJ.: valiera, valieras, valiera, etc.

venir *to come*

PARTICIPLES: *coming*, **viniendo**; *come*, venido.

PRESENT INDICATIVE: *I come, etc.*, **vengo, vienes, viene**; venimos, venís, **vienen**.

IMPERFECT: *I used to come, etc.*, venía, venías, venía, etc.

PAST DEFINITE: *I came etc.*, vine, viniste, vino; vinimos, vinisteis, vinieron.

FUTURE: *I shall come, etc.*, vendré, vendrás, vendrá, etc.

CONDITIONAL: *I should come, etc.*, vendría, vendrías, etc.

IMPERATIVE: *come*, **ven**, venga Vd.; venid, vengan Vds.; *let us come*, vengamos.

PRESENT SUBJ.: venga, vengas, venga, etc.

IMPERFECT SUBJ.: viniese, vinieses, viniese, etc.

FUTURE SUBJ.: viniere, vinieres, viniere, etc.

CONDITIONAL SUBJ.: viniera, vinieras, viniera, etc.

ver *to see*

PARTICIPLES: *seeing*, viendo; *seen*, visto.

PRESENT INDICATIVE: *I see, etc.*, veo, ves, ve; vemos, veis, ven.

IMPERFECT: *I used to see, etc.*, veía, veías, veía; veíamos, veíais veían.

PAST DEFINITE: *I saw, etc.*, vi, viste, vio; vimos, visteis, vieron.

FUTURE: *I shall see, etc.*, veré, verás, verá; veremos, etc.

CONDITIONAL: *I should see, etc.*, vería, verías, vería, etc.

IMPERATIVE: *see*, ve vea Vd.; *ved*, vean Vds.; *let us see*, veamos.

PRESENT SUBJ.: vea, veas, vea; veamos, etc.

IMPERFECT SUBJ.: viese, vieses, viese; viésemos, etc.

FUTURE SUBJ.: viere, vieres, viere; viéremos, etc.

CONDITIONAL SUBJ.: viera, vieras, viera; viéramos, etc.

DEFECTIVE VERBS

There are a few verbs which are not used in all parts of their conjugation. The two chief reasons for this are (*a*) the harsh unpleasant sound which results from certain combinations of letters, and (*b*) the uselessness of certain parts of some verbs, on account of the meaning.

As an example, we may cite *loar* (*to praise*). *Loo* (*I praise*) is supposed not to be used—in fact, like most defective verbs, *loar* is seldom employed, *alabar* being preferred instead. Again, *nacer* (*to be born*) is sometimes classified as defective, because the imperative *be born* is hardly natural or practical phrase.

But as harshness of sound, and the possibility of using certain words and phrases, are both matters of opinion, it necessarily follows that the lists of defective verbs given by different grammarians vary greatly. For instance, *loo* has been used by classic Spanish authors; and even *naced* (*be born*) occurs in an Ode to Spring, where the poet says: *Rosas, naced* (*Roses, be born* = *blossom forth*).

Poder (*to be able to*) can also be classed as defective, it being very unnatural to use this verb in the imperative. But exceptional circumstances arise. It is quite possible to want to say, when instructing a person to display or conceal his ability; *Be able to* (i.e. pretend to be able to) *do so-and-so.*

It therefore follows that a hard and fast line cannot be drawn as regards what parts of certain verbs may be used, or can be used. Fortunately, the matter is of no importance whatever. The defective verbs rarely occur, and foreigners need never use any of them—with the possible exception of *soler* (*to be in the habit of*). When met with in Spanish, no difficulty can arise in translating any part of any verb into English, provided of course that the infinitive is known.

The following list of verbs are those classified as being defective by the Spanish Academy:

aplacer (*to please*). Very rarely used, except in the 3rd person present and imperfect indicative: *aplace, aplacen, aplacía, aplacían.*

atañer (*to appertain*). Only used in the 3rd person, and seldom except in the present indicative: *atañe, atañen.*

balbucir (*to lisp*). Not used in any part of the conjugation where **z** would have to be inserted before the **c** of the stem (see page 65). *Balbucear* is generally used instead of *balbucir*.

concernir (*to concern, relate to*). Only used in the 3rd person, and very rarely except in the present indicative and subjunctive, and in the imperfect indicative: *concierne, conciernen, concierna, conciernan, concernía, concernían.*

soler (*to be wont to, in the habit of*). Used in all persons of the present indicative and subjunctive, and in the imperfect indicative: *suelo, sueles, suele, solemos, soléis, suelen; suela, suelas, suela, solamos, soláis, suelan; solía, solías, solía, solíamos, solíais, solían.* The other tenses rarely occur; the infinitive is not used (except as the name of the verb).

usucapir (*to acquire legal right in property, by lengthy possession*). A legal term, almost unknown except in the infinitive.

The following, and a few other very unusual verbs, are only used in those parts of the conjugation where the termination begins or ends with **i**:

abolir, *to abolish*
aguerrir, *to instruct in military strategy*
arrecirse *and* aterirse, *to become numb with cold*
despavorir, *to be aghast*
embair, *to impose on*
empedernir, *to become petrified*
garantir, *to guarantee*
manir, *to keep meat until it becomes tender*

placer (*to please*) is sometimes classed as defective, and the irregular stems *pleg-* and *plug-* occur. But the Academy advises that unless it is used impersonally, *placer* should be conjugated throughout like the other *-acer* verbs. The 3rd persons are: of past definite, *plugo* or *plació, pluguieron* or *placieron*; of subjunctive present, *plega, plegue* or *plazca*; imperfect *pluguiese* or *placiese*; future *pluguiere* or *placiere*; conditional *pluguiera* or *placiera.*

yacer (*to lie at rest*), although not classified as defective by the Academy, is chiefly used in the 3rd person singular and plural, present indicative. On tombstones, one finds *yace* (*here lies*) and *yacen* (*here lie*). The other parts of this verb are rarely met with.

IMPERSONAL VERBS

Impersonal verbs have no person or thing as their subject, and are only used in the 3rd person singular:

it is raining, *llueve*
will it freeze? *¿helará?*
it is growing dark, *anochece*
it was thundering, *tronaba*
it does not matter, *no importa*
it appears, *parece*

Many impersonal verbs, such as *nevar* (*to snow*), *tronar* (*to thunder*), *helar* (*to freeze*), are necessarily defective; they can only be used in the 3rd person singular.

Impersonal expressions are frequently constructed with *ser*, *hacer*, and other verbs:

it is hot, *hace calor*
it is cold, *hace frío*
it is windy, *hace viento*
it is certain, *es cierto*
it is true, *es verdad*
it is necessary, *es menester*

These phrases can of course be used in any tense, negatively and interrogatively:

will it be windy? *¿hará viento*
it was not true, *no era verdad*

There is, *are*, *was*, *were*, *will be*, etc., are translated by the 3rd person singular of *haber*; but in the present tense *hay* is used instead of *ha*:

there is, there are, *hay*
is there? are there? *¿hay?*
will there be? *¿habrá?*
there is *or* are not, *no hay*
is *or* are there not? *¿no hay?*
there was *or* were not, *no había*

there would be many men, *habría muchos hombres*·
there is no ink *or* there is not any ink, *no hay tinta*
there will not have been time, *no habrá habido tiempo*

(Note that *hay* simply expresses existence; if anything has to be pointed out, *allí esta* (*there is*) or *allí están* (*there are*) is used).

LIST OF THE SPANISH IRREGULAR VERBS

The figures refer to the page on which the conjugation of the verb, or of one similar conjugated, is indicated.

This list does not include regular verbs which have irregular adjectival participles (see pages 68–71). Reflexive verbs, such as *acostarse*, are also omitted, as the conjugation is always the same, whether the verb is used reflexively or not. For this reason, infinitives only are given, without the addition of the pronoun 'se'; but some of the infinitives in this list, such as *arrepentir*, are only used reflectively.

* conjugated like *pedir* (page 92). † conjugated like *cerrar* (page 54)
(Verbs marked *, †, are omitted from the lists on pages 56 to 64)

* conjugated like *perder* (page 54) † conjugated like *cerrar* (page 96)

* conjugated like *costar* (page 55)

SOME OTHER **HUGO** PUBLICATIONS

If you cannot get our books and audio courses from your local bookseller, write to us at 104 Judd Street, London WC1H 9NF. We will send details of titles currently in print, prices and other information.

THREE MONTHS BOOKS are available in French, German, Spanish, Italian, Greek, Portuguese, Dutch, Norwegian, Danish, Swedish, Russian and Latin. Using the world-famous Hugo method of self-tuition and imitated pronunciation, these books are as suitable for beginners as they are for those with a basic knowledge of the language (the latter will find them excellent for revision purposes).

AUDIO COURSES in French, German, Spanish, Italian, Dutch, Greek, Portuguese and Swedish, based on the appropriate 'Three Months' book. These Courses represent one of the most up-to-date concepts in modern language-learning techniques. Designed to take beginners through to a good working knowledge of both the spoken and the written language, they will also benefit the more proficient student who needs to revise. A fully descriptive leaflet is available, giving details of cassettes and records. Also produced (at present in French, German, Spanish and Italian only) are more advanced colloquial Conversation Cassette/book packs in the "Speak — Today!" series.

VERB BOOKS in French, German, Italian and Spanish; these are essential reference books for 'Three Months' students. Among other aids to learning the most important part of any language are lists of irregular verbs and model conjugations of auxiliaries and regular verbs.

POCKET DICTIONARIES contain a minimum of 22,000 words each, with every headword given its imitated pronunciation. These handy books (in French, German, Spanish, Italian, Russian and Dutch) are invaluable for both tourists and businessmen. There is also a pocket English Dictionary (25,000 entries approx.) without pronunciation.

PHRASE BOOKS for France, Germany, Spain, Italy, Portugal, Holland, Greece and Scandinavia (Norway, Denmark and Sweden in one). An ample selection of words and phrases with imitated pronunciation is coupled with information on each subject heading ('Hotels', 'Motoring' etc.). In addition, there is a brief background to the country, its habits and customs.

GB £ NET +000.95

ISBN 0-85285-022-0

00095

9 780852 850220